NON-EXECUTIVE DIRECTORS' CHECKLISTS

Mark Wearden

Chartered
Governance
Institute
UK & Ireland

Published by
CGI Publishing Limited
Saffron House, 6–10 Kirby Street
London EC1N 8TS

Typeset by Paul Barrett Book Production, Cambridge
Edited by Benedict O'Hagan
Cover designed by Anthony Kearney

British Library Cataloguing in Publication Data
A catalogue record for this book is available from the British Library.

ISBN 978-1-86072-793-1

Table of contents

About the author

Mark delivers consultancy projects through MBS Governance, a private strategy consultancy, which he has run for the past 25 years following 12 years in International Banking as an analyst, and 8 years in industry as a finance director.

In addition to his client-focused consultancy, Mark is an experienced non-executive director and an audit committee advisor. He undertakes director and board mentoring, a range of academic work, and delivers public workshops, seminars and lectures for professional bodies, together with in-house programmes for boards and directors.

Until December 2019 Mark was The Chartered Governance Institute's strategy examiner and an assessor for The Institute's final level exams. In addition to authoring the The Institute's *Development of Strategy* textbook Mark is a member of the judging panel for The Institute's annual reporting awards

Mark has worked extensively with directors and senior managers from a wide range of organisations, from FTSE 100 down and back again, giving him a challenging insight into the minds of the directors of corporate Britain. He specialises in strategic analysis and challenge, aligned with board and director evaluation. In 2019 he stepped down as Chairman of the Association of Chartered Certified Accountants (ACCA) Global Forum on Governance, Risk and Performance after two years.

In addition to authoring the Wolters Kluwer/Croner-i *Practical Guide for Audit Committees*, Mark writes regular eCPD modules and articles for Croner-i. His areas of research and interest are 'governance thinking', 'risk and reporting', 'financial analysis', 'supply chain challenge' and exploring the dichotomy that frequently exists between theory and practice.

Acknowledgements

I offer thanks to the plethora of people who I have worked with over the years. They have endured my challenges, questioning and lateral thinking, and have helped me develop an understanding of why it is only ever the people that matter within an organisation. It is these people who determine success or failure, but it is their very humanity and irrationality which requires some measure of governance and challenge.

If the role of director – executive and non-executive – has a value, it is based on the ability to always step back and place human behaviour and decision making within the organisational and wider stakeholder context. I thank all those directors, and others who have spent time with me, for their mutually challenging perceptions.

I offer sincere thanks to Saqib and Ben at The Chartered Governance Institute who have worked with me on bringing this text to fruition and, in particular, for their understanding and ongoing support during some challenging times. In this same regard, I also offer my thanks, and those of the Institute, to Catherine Wright Davies who has added significantly to the completeness and completion of this text.

Most importantly, I give heartfelt thanks to my wife Marian for her patience, belief, challenge and love across many years; without her constant support my eclectic approach to work would have been impossible.

Acronyms

ACCA	Association of Chartered Certified Accountants
AGM	annual general meeting
AI	artificial intelligence
AIM	Alternative Investment Market
ARGA	Audit, Reporting and Governance Authority
BEIS	Department for Business, Energy and Industrial Strategy
CA 2006	Companies Act 2006
CEO	chief executive officer
CFO	chief financial officer
COSO	Committee of Sponsoring Organizations of the Treadway Commission
CPS	Crown Prosecution Service
CSR	corporate social responsibility
D&O	directors and officers (insurance)
DTR	Disclosure and Transparency Rules
EBITDA	earnings before interest, taxes, depreciation and amortisation
ED	executive director
EGM	extraordinary general meeting
EPIC	Embankment Project for Inclusive Capital
ERM	enterprise resource management
ESG	environmental, social and governance issues
FCA	Financial Conduct Authority
FRC	Financial Reporting Council
FRS	Financial Reporting Standard
GAAP	Generally Accepted Accounting Principles
GDPR	General Data Protection Regulation
HMRC	Her Majesty's Revenue and Customs
IAS	International Accounting Standard
IBE	Institute of Business Ethics
ICO	Information Commissioner's Office
IFRS	International Financial Reporting Standards
IIRC	International Integrated Reporting Council
INED	independent non-executive director
KPI	key performance indicators
MAR	EU Market Abuse Regulation
NED	non-executive director
NI	National Insurance
PAYE	pay as you earn

PSC	person with significant control
QCA	Quoted Companies Alliance
RLE	relevant legal entity
SAIL	Single Alternative Inspection Location
SID	senior independent director
TBL	triple bottom line
TCFD	Task Force on Climate-related Financial Disclosures
ToR	terms of reference
VAT	value added tax

Introduction

Non-executive directors (NEDs) play a fundamental and increasingly important role in the governance of a company. Independence of thought and action is a duty expected from all directors, but the non-executive director should be able to bring an additional and challenging objectivity and independence through their lack of involvement in the day-to-day, habitual operational activities of an organisation. They need to have the ability to be able to 'see the wood through the trees'.

These checklists for non-executive directors are designed to deliver a number of differing stimuli.

- Clarity of understanding.
- Reminder of key requirements.
- Questions to challenge self and others.

These checklists are neither prescriptive nor exclusive. They will not all be relevant to every non-executive director and they do not cover everything that a non-executive director needs to know. However, I am confident that there will be something challenging contained herein for every non-executive director. The book should be used to sense-check specific aspects or to dip in and challenge oneself.

Every organisation is different, and every director is different.

There is very rarely, if ever, only one right answer in the world of corporate governance. Likewise, there is never only one right answer in the interpretation of the finances of an organisation.

Non-executive directors, in particular, need to take the time to understand and consider the breadth of possible answers before decisions are taken around the board table.

My experience of working with many boards and many directors suggests two gaps that are often evidenced in the boardroom.

- Lack of financial literacy – the ability to look at, read, consider and challenge a set of figures. After all, they underpin the liquidity and viability of the company.

- Lack of professional scepticism – the ability to step back and challenge what is being presented from a perspective which eliminates bias.

It is important to enjoy the role of non-executive director, but it is not for the faint-hearted.

Mark Wearden MSc FCCA FCIS

Annual general meeting

Introduction

A private company does not need to hold an annual general meeting (AGM) unless the constitution requires this to happen. All procedural matters for general meetings (notice period, voting etc) will usually form part of the articles of association of the company.

A public company must hold an AGM within six months of its accounting reference date. Where a company's accounting reference period is shortened, the AGM must be held within three months of the giving of the notice to shorten the accounting period. A public company may not need to hold an AGM in any particular calendar year if it has a financial year in excess of 12 months.

The 'ordinary' business of the AGM is to:

- receive the most recent accounts;
- consider the remuneration report (quoted companies only);
- confirm the declaration of a final dividend (where appropriate);
- approve the remuneration of the auditors; and
- re-elect the auditors and retiring directors, if necessary.

Any other business is deemed to be 'special' business. The majority of the following points are therefore applicable directly to public companies with their AGM requirement but may also be of use as reference points to companies who choose to have an AGM.

NED checklist

- Is the AGM being held within the required time (i.e. six months of the financial year end for plcs)?
- Is there a final proposed dividend payment which needs AGM approval?
- Does the directors' remuneration report need to be approved at an AGM (this is obligatory for a listed company)?

- Is the appointment and reappointment of directors clear and does it require approval at an AGM? Will the board balance continue to remain appropriate and in line with any code, shareholder or stakeholder expectations?

Procedure

- The company secretary will normally handle all matters pertaining to an AGM but a NED, as a director, needs to be satisfied that:
  - the correct notice has been given to members of the company;
  - that the notice of AGM, any proposed resolutions, and any required voting (including the use of a proxy) have been prepared and circulated within the required timescales;
  - the timing and venue for the AGM is appropriate for the expected attendance to ensure an appropriate opportunity for challenge and debate if required; and
  - all communications are clear and appropriate for maintaining the reputation of the company.

Notes

- Remember that an AGM is an annual meeting for the owners to maintain their oversight of the control of their investment.
- The procedural requirements for any additional 'general' meetings of shareholders, historically referred to as extraordinary general meetings (EGM), will be covered in the Companies Act 2006 (CA2006) and/or the constitution of the company – as with the AGM.

Annual report and accounts

Introduction

All UK limited companies (ltd and plc) are required to submit a report to Companies House and to their shareholders at least annually, underpinned by the financial statements dated at the end of each financial year of the company.

The contents and format of the financial, non-financial and narrative aspects of the report are determined by the size and nature of the company concerned.

The report is signed by a named director of the company on behalf of each director of the company.

Traditionally, such reports have been viewed as an historic report of the directors to the shareholders as at the year-end date. Driven, at least partly, by the strategic report expectations within CA2006, reports for all companies except small companies now contain a greater level of strategic projection and commentary from the directors. Combined with enhanced stakeholder awareness and the speed of media and social media communication, this has led to year-end reports being viewed by many as a future-looking as well as a historic report. This perspective, and such a reliance, has not yet been tested in law.

NED checklist

- Understand the reporting requirements for the size of company of which you are a NED, remembering that the report is issued in your name.
- Enquire and have confidence in the process that leads to the production of the final annual report and accounts – where there is extensive narrative, who is the compiler and author? The call from shareholders is for a more focused and combined approach to reporting, not just a series of separate reports.
- As a director, do you have the opportunity to review financial, non-financial and narrative aspects of the report in sufficient time to enable constructive challenge and input, if required?

- Ensure that the final version is debated by all directors during a formal minuted board meeting, and the appropriate resolution is approved to put the report and accounts to the members for approval in the AGM.

Requirements

- Small and micro companies under CA2006:
  - minimum financial information of balance sheet at year-end date, with any appropriate notes; and
  - a short and formulaic directors' report.
- Medium-sized companies under CA2006:
  - more detailed financial information including an income statement and cashflow statement to supplement the balance sheet;
  - a directors' report;
  - a limited strategic report; and
  - an auditor's report.
- Large private companies under CA2006:
  - detailed financial information;
  - a directors' report;
  - a detailed strategic report, including an increasing range of wider stakeholder and corporate social responsibility (CSR) information; and
  - an auditor's report.
- Larger private companies under CA2006 as enhanced by the Companies (Miscellaneous Reporting) Regulations 2018:
  - all the requirements for 'large' companies; and
  - governance reporting using either the Wates Principles or an acceptable alternative on an 'apply or explain' basis.
- Public listed companies:
  - all the requirements for 'large' companies; and
  - governance and other reporting in accordance with the requirements of the Listing Rules: currently, the application of the UK Corporate Governance Code 2018 on a 'comply or explain' basis.

Notes

- Always remember that the Companies Act requires the annual report and accounts to be 'consistent with the size and complexity of the business'.

Further information

- The Chartered Governance Institute: guidance note: 'Contents list for the annual report of a UK company'.

Appointment to the board

Introduction

The required procedure for a director to be appointed to a particular company will be contained within the constitution of the company. Achieving the optimal balance of directors on the board of the company will contribute significantly to the efficacy, effectiveness, viability and sustainability of the company.

Principle J of the UK Corporate Governance Code suggests:

> Appointments to the board should be subject to a formal, rigorous and transparent procedure, and an effective succession plan should be maintained for board and senior management. Both appointments and succession plans should be based on merit and objective criteria and within this context, should promote diversity of gender social and ethnic backgrounds, cognitive and personal strengths.

Principle K suggests:

> The board and its committees should have a combination of skills, experience and knowledge. Consideration should be given to the length of service of the board as a whole and membership regularly refreshed.

While these principles and the Code apply specifically to listed companies, it can be argued that the logic and thinking behind them are applicable to all limited companies, at a level appropriate to the size and complexity of a company.

NED checklist

- Each director must be willing to accept their appointment as either an executive director (ED) or a NED.
- The contractual terms for the appointment of a director should be agreed before the matter is considered formally by either the board of directors or the shareholders.
- The expectation in terms of number of meetings, number of additional days, other associated duties, and preparation time should

be discussed, agreed and included in the letter of appointment or service contract.

- Before accepting an appointment as a NED, it is important that the prospective director should undertake an appropriate level of due diligence with regard to the company and its reputation. The Chartered Governance Institute Guidance Note on Due Diligence suggests:

  > by making the right enquiries, asking the right questions and taking care to understand the replies, a prospective director can reduce the risk of nasty surprises and dramatically increase the likelihood of succes.

Procedure

- The articles of association will usually include provisions that allow for:
  - the minuted agreement by existing directors at a board meeting to appoint a person who is willing to act as a director;
  - the appointed person will hold office until the next AGM;
  - a resolution will be presented to the shareholders at that AGM proposing the appointment of the person as a director; and
  - in a private company where the shareholders have elected not to hold an AGM, new directors are generally elected by a written resolution from the shareholders.

Requirements

- The appointment of a director to any limited company should be notified to Companies House within 14 days of the appointment using (electronically) form AP01, this will usually be carried out by the company secretary.
- A listed company is required by the UK Listing Rules to announce any new appointment of a director to the stock market, stating whether it is an appointment of an executive director, a NED, and/or the chair of the company.
- CA2006 s. 228 requires a copy of the service contract of each director to be available for inspection at either the company's registered office or the Single Alternative Inspection Location (SAIL) address.

Further information

- The Chartered Governance Institute: guidance note, 'Sample non-executive director's appointment letter'.

Articles of association

The articles of association (articles) are the rules governing a company's internal affairs. They are often referred to as the constitution of the company and are generally based on a standard set of principles for the operation of a company.

Companies incorporated prior to 1 October 2009 will have as their default articles the version of Table A (or model articles) in force when the company was incorporated; later versions of Table A do not apply unless specifically adopted by a company.

Companies incorporated on or after 1 October 2009 will have as their default the model articles from Companies House, unless these are excluded or varied by the company's own articles.

NED checklist

- A copy of the articles should be included in the induction material available for all NEDs.
- Are the articles 'fit for purpose'? These are the 'rules of engagement' for the directors of the company. Do they reflect the 21st century status of the company and are they written in clear and understandable modern English?
- Is the procedure for director appointment clear and has it been followed correctly?
- Is the procedure for calling and operation of directors' meetings followed in accordance with the articles?
- Is the quorum for directors' meetings realistic, workable and as required?
- Is it clear how directors of the company are expected to behave? Are there any particular expectations for this company?
- Are there any special shareholder provisions that a NED needs to be aware of?

Procedures

- To amend the articles of a company, a directors' board meeting would usually recommend changes to the members of the company through presenting a resolution at an AGM or an EGM. In the case of a private company, this can be circulated as a written resolution unless disallowed through either the articles or previous resolution.
- Any change to the articles is classed as a special resolution and must therefore contain the full text of any and all proposed changes.
- If the articles are to be changed through an AGM or EGM, it is important to ensure that the meeting is quorate and any necessary majority is attained to pass the resolution.

Filing requirement

- An initial set of articles are filed to form a company. By default, these are the model articles, but can be amended at the outset by those forming the company, or thereafter by special resolution of the shareholders.
- A signed copy of any special resolution amending the articles must be filed at Companies House within 15 days, together with a copy of the amended articles and a signed copy of the resolution.

Notes

- Articles may contain entrenched provisions, such as a general over riding principle with regard to members or dividends or an underlying ethos and principle of operation of the company. An amendment to an entrenched provision requires either 100% consent from members entitled to vote or a court order.

Further information

- Current versions of the model articles, appropriate for private companies limited by shares, private companies limited by guarantee and public companies are available from the Companies House website (see www.gov.uk/guidance/model-articles-of-association-for-limited-companies).
- Checklist: Directors' Duties – Duty one, page 103.

Artificial intelligence

Introduction

The industrial and commercial world within which we operate is described as entering the fourth industrial revolution, a technological revolution that will fundamentally alter the way we live, work and relate to each other. It is suggested that its scale, scope and complexity will be unlike anything that people have ever experienced. Precisely how it will evolve is an unknown unknown, but it will involve all aspects of our lives.

The first industrial revolution mechanised production through the use of water and steam power, the second used electricity to create mass production, the third used electronics and information technology to automate production.

The fourth revolution is blurring the lines between physical, digital and biological spheres, causing:

- disruption to jobs and skills;
- the need for greater innovation and enhanced productivity;
- greater inequalities amongst people;
- agility in governance;
- breakdowns in security;
- enhanced risks to data through cyber crime;
- business disruption;
- technology fusion; and
- challenges to ethics and perceived societal norms.

Much of this is typified by the rapidly encroaching use of artificial intelligence (AI). This is no longer a future concern for directors of companies; this is a reality of today. A recent McKinsey report suggested that a fifth of the global workforce could lose their jobs to AI by 2030, but we saw similar threats with regard to the dramatic changes in working practice brought about through the internet.

The role of the NED is to bring a challenging and governance-based perspective to how AI is, can, and should be used to help to drive success for shareholders and stakeholders.

NED checklist

- How, where and when is AI used within the organisation and/or its supply chain?
- Who owns the oversight and control of AI within the organisation?
- Is AI (existing and potential) included within the risk register or other means of debating and challenging organisational risk?
- Who in the organisation understands the algorithms, models and data that is incorporated in any AI usage? Is this left just to external agencies?
- Are audit, risk and compliance functions within the organisation involved in all aspects of AI projects to ensure appropriate oversight and control?
- Is the board as a whole cognisant of all matters relating to AI within the organisation?
- Has the actual and potential 'people' impact of AI within the organisation been considered? Is this included in CA2006 s. 172 reporting from the directors?
- Are the NEDs encouraged to bring an independent challenge and scepticism to the AI debate within the organisation?

Procedure

- Identify current and future use of AI within the organisation and its supply chain.
- Consider the material risk impact of the use of such AI.
- Ensure that AI is a regular feature on the board agenda and is included as appropriate within consideration of strategy, risk and control.

Assurance

Introduction

The role of all directors is to give assurance to the shareholders (and stakeholders) that the company is being run in their best interests, as a going concern and from the perspective of longer-term viability.

The dictionary definition of the word 'assurance' is:

> a positive declaration intended to give confidence; a promise.

This underpins the core thrust of the second of the statutory duties of a director (CA2006 s. 172) with its new associated reporting expectations:

> A director of a company must act in the way he considers, in good faith, would be most likely to promote the success of the company for the benefit of its members as a whole.

Remember that 'assurance' is effectively a communication process involving two or more human brains, so it is important to allow for bias and skew in the compilation, transmission and interpretation of data and information.

NED checklist

- Consider, understand and challenge the different lines of assurance that exist i.e. those assurances going up, down and across the organisation and outside of the organisation. Are they effective and efficient?
- Is the corporate communication appropriately robust to allow the level of integrity required to deliver assurance?
- Given that assurance is a person-to-person communication process, how well do you know and understand the people that you rely upon to give you assurance and, in particular, their biases and integrity? Remember that you will be judged in the same manner by those to whom you give assurance.

Requirements

- Directors sit in a pivotal and legally accountable role with regard to assurance. This is evidenced in a number of different corporate relationships:
  - shareholders and stakeholders expect assurance from the directors of the company;
  - directors expect assurance from the senior management and others within the company in the form of regular, focused and accurate written verbal reports;
  - NEDs expect assurance from the executive directors and other senior management of the company; and
  - there is a mutual relationship of assurance between directors and external auditors.

Audit – auditor requirement

Introduction

All limited companies, other than companies classed as small under CA2006, are required to appoint external auditors and prepare audited accounts. Even if a company is exempt from audit, by size, a resolution supported by at least 10% of its members may require it to appoint auditors.

Directors of a company will usually decide upon and select an appropriate firm of auditors and then propose such firm to the shareholders in general meeting.

If a company that is required to have its accounts audited fails to appoint auditors, notification must be sent to the Secretary of State; the Secretary of State may appoint auditors to fill the vacancy.

An auditor is required to be registered as an auditor and must not be an officer or a servant of the company, or a partner or employee of such officers or servants. An auditor may be an individual, a partnership or a limited company.

The process and product of audit is under considerable review and scrutiny following a number of corporate failures, the challenges being whether the current approach to audit is 'fit for purpose' and whether the audit market is too dominated by the 'big four' audit firms.

It is important that a NED remains fully aware of changes in the law and expectation with regard to audit and auditors.

NED checklist

- Does the company qualify for exemption from audit?
- Has an audit been requested by more than 10% of members?
- Have the directors undertaken an appropriately rigorous selection process for their recommendation to members of an auditor?
- Is the proposed auditor appropriately qualified, of suitable size and experience for the company, with knowledge of the sector and markets within which the company operates?

Procedure

- Determine the need for an audit, together with the experience and size of auditor appropriate to the size and complexity of the organisation.
- Formalise the proposal at a meeting of the whole board.
- Take a resolution to the members of the company to approve the appointment of the auditor.

Requirement

- Refer to the checklist: Audit – external audit, page 17.

Notes

- A small company under CA2006 meets at least two of the following criteria:
  - an annual turnover of no more than £10.2 million;
  - assets worth no more than £5.1 million; or
  - 50 or fewer employees on average.
- When an audit committee exists, this would be the usual forum for the initial consideration and proposal of an auditor. The audit committee being a proposal to the whole board for the forming of a resolution to the members.

Further information

- ICSA Publishing: The Non-Executive Directors' Handbook, Chapter 6: 'The Audit Committee' (2019).

Audit – external audit

Introduction

When a company is required to submit audited accounts, they must appoint an appropriately qualified external auditor. The concept of 'external' being that such an auditor is independent from the company and able to undertake a professional, unbiased and objective appraisal of the finances and financial state of the company.

Amongst other areas, an external auditor is required to:

- consider whether the accounts of the company give a 'true and fair' view of the company's finances at the date of the balance sheet;
- identify and assess the risk of material misstatement;
- assess and confirm whether the company is a going concern;
- review the financial policies applied;
- consider the reasonableness of material estimates, judgements and their related disclosures;
- assess whether the levels of internal control are appropriate and robust; and
- whether all appropriate financial reporting standards have been followed and applied.

The external auditors are appointed or reappointed on an annual basis by the members of the company in a general meeting. The accounts are audited as a statutory requirement and on behalf of the members.

However, the majority of the practical work undertaken during the external work will be carried out with the executive directors, senior management and employees of the business.

The independent role of the NED is therefore paramount in this process to consider and challenge whether an audit has been carried out with appropriate independence, robustness and scepticism.

The UK Corporate Governance Code 2018 advises the audit committee is delegated to review the effectiveness of the external audit process. When an audit committee does not exist, it is appropriate for NEDs to review the external audit separately from the executive directors.

The external audit process, intensity and level of NED involvement should be aligned to the size, complexity and risks of the organisation.

NED checklist

- Does the audit committee take the governance oversight lead on external audit?
- If an audit committee does not exist, how do the NEDs ensure an appropriate level of external auditor scrutiny and challenge?
- Are the NEDs involved appropriately in all aspects of the external audit cycle?
- Has the external auditor been selected and approved in a correct manner?
- Does the board receive confirmation each year of the independence and objectivity of the external audit firm, and of the people practically involved in the audit process?
- Do you, as a NED, have confidence in the lead auditor, and in the robustness of the audit process?
- When did the board last change external auditor?

Procedure

- Selection of the auditors, followed by proposal from the board and approval by the members.
- A formal engagement letter should set out the expectations from both sides and the fee that will be payable.
- An audit planning meeting (or series of meetings, if necessary) should be held between the auditors, the senior finance team and the audit committee to determine levels of materiality and core focus areas for the year. If appropriate, there might be an additional meeting at this stage between the audit committee and the auditors without executive management or senior employees present. A similar meeting should be held later after the audit process has started, as and when necessary.
- The audit takes place. Dependent on the size of company, an interim or pre-emptive systems audit may take place to ensure a timely year-end process.
- The initial report and findings should be discussed with relevant parties. This should include a review meeting between external auditors and audit committee without any executive directors or senior management present.

- The auditor's report is received by the company, and the report and accounts are finalised and approved by the board of directors. Action points should be noted by the audit committee.
- The audited accounts are presented to the members of the company at the AGM, usually with the external auditor present.

Further information

- ICSA Publishing: The Non-Executive Directors' Handbook, Chapter 6: 'The Audit Committee' (2019).

Audit – internal audit

Introduction

Internal audit is widely recognised as a core function that is required within an organisation to oversee, monitor, assess, and provide assurance across a wide range of financial and non-financial systems and structures.

The precise nature and extent of the work carried out by internal audit will vary widely between different organisations. The provision of internal audit is neither a statutory nor a codified requirement. Many organisations, even those of a reasonable size, do not have a formal internal audit function, but instead rely upon other oversight mechanisms within internal control systems to provide evidence and assurance to the board that systems are in place and are working.

Provision 25 of the UK Corporate Governance Code includes the following expectation for the roles and responsibilities of an audit committee:

> monitoring and reviewing the effectiveness of the company's internal audit function or, where there is not one, considering annually whether there is a need for one and making a recommendation to the board.

This underlines the principle of internal audit – an internal means of taking a step back and considering the various systems and processes which exist to mitigate risk and ensure due process is followed. If this is not done formally through an internal audit process, the directors need to still be assured that somehow it is happening.

NED checklist

- Is there an internal audit function?
- If not, then why not? How do you, as a NED, receive assurance on control processes?
- If an internal audit function exists:
  - Does it report directly to the board or the audit committee (if one exists)?

- How do they know whether it is effective?
- How is the function structured, and is it appropriate for the size and complexity of the business?
- When was it last reviewed?
- Who does the internal auditor report to?
- Who decides the internal audit agenda?

Procedure

If internal audit is an internal (employee-based) function its attributes are:

- Positive – continual presence, high visibility, cultural understanding, familiarity, direct line accountability.
- Negative – part of the structure and system, loss of objectivity, familiarity, conflicts of interest.

If internal audit is an external (outsourced) function its attributes are:

- Positive – focused, objective, self-managing, specialist activity, independent challenge.
- Negative – agenda-based, high-level, remote, risk of 'tick-box' approach.

Requirements

- Where there is no internal audit function, the board of directors, as a whole, should review the need for one on an annual basis.
- If an internal audit function exists (employee-based or outsourced) the reporting lines of accountability should be clear. The purpose is objectivity and challenge.

Notes

- There is no right answer as to the optimal internal audit structure. This will depend entirely on the organisational and structure requirements, aligned with the skill set, financial and technical literacy of the people involved throughout the risk and control function within each individual organisation.

Further information

- ICSA Publishing: The Non-Executive Directors' Handbook, Chapter 10: 'Internal control and risk management' (2019).

Audit committee

Introduction

The audit committee has a key role in ensuring effective corporate governance. It is the pivotal point for the recognition and monitoring of risk, appropriateness of financial and narrative reporting, and assurance that controls are in place to protect the viability and sustainability of the organisation.

Under Principle 24 of the Code:

> The board should establish an audit committee of independent non-executive directors, with a minimum membership of three, or in the case of smaller companies, two. The chair of the board should not be a member. The board should satisfy itself that at least one member has recent and relevant financial experience. The committee as a whole shall have competence relevant to the sector in which the company operates.

Despite its central role in effective governance, an audit committee, like any other committee appointed by a board of directors, is a committee of the board. All directors of an organisation continue to hold unitary responsibility for the governance and control of that organisation.

NED checklist

- Do you have an audit committee? If not, do you regularly review the need for an audit committee?
- Do you feel competent to serve on an audit committee? If not, then build your financial literacy.
- How do you monitor risk and control within your organisation?
- If you have an internal audit function, are they effective? If you have no internal audit function, where does the 'control', oversight and responsibility for this function lie?
- How close is the interaction with the external auditors? When were the audit partner of the external auditors last rotated or a tender process undertaken? Is their agenda appropriate to your

organisation today? Are you aware of their materiality levels, business focus, judgements? Do we meet with the external auditors without executive directors or management being present?

- Who writes the narrative in your report and accounts? Does it align with and explain the financial reporting? Remember it is the report of the directors to the shareholders.
- Does your audit committee agenda and number of meetings allow enough time for robust challenge and the fulfilment of your responsibilities?
- Do we report regularly to the full board of directors to ensure that they are aware of our scrutiny and oversight? Remember that financial accountability lies with each and every director.

Procedure

- Ensure that the terms of reference for the audit committee are up-to-date and regularly reviewed.
- Ensure that an appropriate level of financial literacy exists around the audit committee table.
- Ensure that members are appointed to the audit committee in line with the constitution and have the appropriate skill, knowledge, and experience.
- As a committee you need to be confident in challenging all aspects of internal financial controls, internal controls and risk management systems and reporting, together with being prepared to challenge the external auditors. Remember, the majority of financial judgements are based upon opinion; there is rarely only one right answer.

Requirements

The UK Corporate Governance Code includes the following list of responsibilities for an audit committee and this is a good guide to the breadth of expectation. A NED should be satisfied that, if the audit committee is not carrying out any of these roles, they are certain who is. As with other references in this book, the Code is seen as having significant relevance far beyond the requirements of listed companies. All these audit committee responsibilities need to happen in any company requiring an external audit:

- monitoring the integrity of the financial statements of the company and any formal announcements relating to the company's financial performance, and reviewing significant financial reporting judgements contained within them;
- providing advice (where requested by the board) on whether the annual report and accounts, taken as a whole, is fair, balanced and understandable, and provides the information necessary for

shareholders to assess the company's position and performance, business model and strategy;

- reviewing the company's internal financial controls and internal control and risk management systems, unless expressly addressed by a separate board risk committee composed of independent non-executive directors or by the board itself;
- monitoring and reviewing the effectiveness of the company's internal audit function or, where there is not one, considering annually whether there is a need for one and making a recommendation to the board;
- conducting the tender process and making recommendations to the board, about the appointment, reappointment and removal of the external auditor, and approving the remuneration and terms of engagement of the external auditor;
- reviewing and monitoring the external auditor's independence and objectivity;
- reviewing the effectiveness of the external audit process, taking into consideration relevant UK professional and regulatory requirements;
- developing and implementing policy on the engagement of the external auditor to supply non-audit services, ensuring there is prior approval of non-audit services, considering the impact this may have on independence, taking into account the relevant regulations and ethical guidance in this regard, and reporting to the board on any improvement or action required; and
- reporting to the board on how it has discharged its responsibilities.

Further information

- Financial Reporting Council (FRC): Guidance on Audit Committees, (2016).
- The Chartered Governance Institute: guidance note, 'terms of reference for an audit committee'.
- FRC: UK Corporate Governance Code (2018).
- ICSA Publishing: The Non-Executive Directors' Handbook – Chapter 6, 'The Audit Committee' (2019).

Audit Reporting and Governance Authority (ARGA)

Introduction

Following several corporate failures in 2017 and 2018 (including BHS and Carillion) the Department for Business, Energy and Industrial Strategy (BEIS) commissioned three separate committee reviews into corporate regulation and the oversight of audit, auditors and the audit market.

Led by Sir John Kingman, the committee was asked to review the work and regulation of the Financial Reporting Council (FRC), with the view of evolving a new regulator that would be 'a beacon for the best in governance, transparency, and independence'.

The Kingman review findings contained 83 recommendations for change and many discussions with relevant stakeholders were held before final decisions and changes were made. The most significant change proposed by the Kingman review is the replacement of the FRC as soon as possible with a new regulator to be known as the Audit, Reporting and Governance Authority (ARGA), summarised as follows:

A new regulator
The Audit, Reporting and Governance Authority should be an independent regulator, accountable to Parliament and to the Department for Business, Energy and Industrial Strategy (BEIS). It should have the following strategic objective and operational duties:

Strategic objective

To protect the interests of investors and the wider public interest by setting high standards of corporate governance, corporate reporting and statutory audit, and by holding to account the companies and professional advisers responsible for meeting those standards.

Operational duties

In pursuing its strategic objective, it must act in a way that:

- is forward looking, seeking to anticipate and where possible act on emerging corporate governance, reporting or audit risks, both in the short and the longer term;

- promotes competition in the market for statutory audit services;
- advances innovation and continuous quality improvements;
- promotes brevity, comprehensibility and usefulness in corporate reporting;
- is proportionate, having regard to the size and resources of those being regulated and balancing the costs and benefits of regulatory action;
- is collaborative, working closely with other regulators both in the UK and internationally; and
- prioritises regulatory activity on the basis of risk, having regard to the Regulators' Code.

The fundamental change here is accountability. ARGA is to be directly accountable to the UK Parliament through BEIS and will have significant powers and oversight. It has been generally accepted by the UK government and the market stakeholders that this change should occur; the transition process has already started. The precise timing of many of the implications will be determined by the UK government in due course.

NED checklist

- What are the implications for your company of a change from voluntary regulation to statutory regulation within the audit market?
- As a NED, if challenged by a regulator, could you defend the approach of your company and its directors to the oversight, mitigation and control of risk within the organisation, from both an internal and an external audit perspective?
- Ensure that you have a means of keeping up to date with the latest changes in the oversight and regulation of companies and that you and your fellow directors consider the implication for your company on a regular basis.

Further information

- Checklist: Financial Reporting Council, page 149.
- Independent Review of the Financial Reporting Council (Kingman Review) 2018. Available at: assets.publishing.service.gov.uk/government/uploads/system/uploads/attachment_data/file/767387/frc-independent-review-final-report.pdf.

Balanced Scorecard

Introduction

Writing in the *Harvard Business Review*, Kaplan and Norton (1992) first developed the concept of the Balanced Scorecard.

A Balanced Scorecard approach is in common usage in many organisations and is usually a derivation of the original work of Kaplan and Norton. This framework for strategy development suggests that organisations should consider future strategic requirements (leading indicators), in addition to financial performance (a lagging indicator) which tends to be backwards facing. In order for an organisation to establish whether it is on course to achieving its strategic objectives, a balance of indicators and measures in four different but complementary perspectives can be used. These are discussed below.

Strategic thinking in the boardroom requires directors to challenge the quantitative nature of financial thinking alongside other qualitative aspects of organisation dynamics and culture.

The balanced scorecard takes a structured approach which requires us to consider our organisation as it exists and is perceived today. This will then allow us to better understand and challenge the strategic changes envisaged.

The original model uses the following four perspectives, but it is important to find the right perspectives for the particular idiosyncrasies and drivers of any organisation. Many organisations either amend the perspectives to suit their own particular organisational circumstances or extend the perspectives to include more than four dimensions (be warned: do not have too many or you lose the purpose of a focused business model).

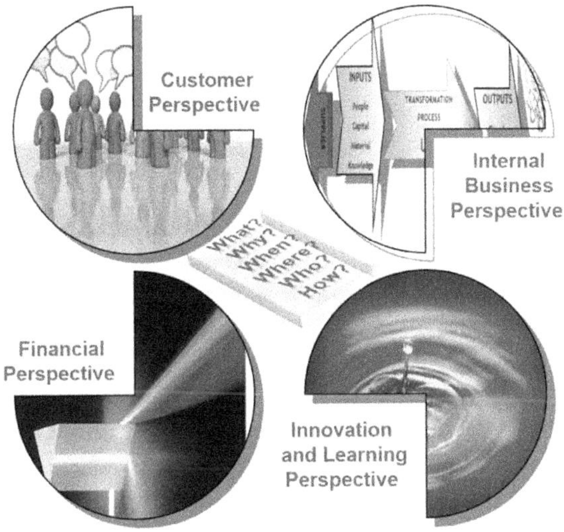

NED checklist

Using the Kaplan and Norton perspectives you should (or could) ask the following questions:

- Customer perspective:
  - What do your customers think of you, why do they buy from you, will they continue to buy from you?
- Internal business perspective:
  - What do you look like from the inside, are you efficient, what do your employees say about you, what does your culture look like, what do you need to do to achieve your customer goals?
- Innovation and learning perspective:
  - What does your business look like today, is it always changing, has it stayed still for too long, when did you last change the way you do things, how seriously are you taking the technological challenges in the short term (three to five years) and long term (10–20 years or more)?
- Financial perspective:
  - How robust is your financial infrastructure, what are your key financial objectives (i.e. revenue, profit, cost savings and efficiencies, profit margins, revenue sources)? What could make you fail (one aspect going wrong, or a concatenation of aspects)? Do your key players have their respective fingers on the financial pulse of the organisation? How do these measures align and associate with shareholder and stakeholder perceptions of the business?

Requirements

The Balanced Scorecard is a strategy execution tool which helps companies:

- clarify strategy by communication and articulating their business objectives and priorities;
- monitor progress by measuring the extent to which the objectives and priorities are being delivered; and
- manage and define action plans which deliver the priorities and objectives by ensuring initiatives and activities are in place.

Even if your company does not use a Balanced Scorecard approach, as a NED it is important to ensure that you have access to a range of different views, feedback and perspectives of the company, not just view the company using key performance indicators (KPIs) and statistics. The Balanced Scorecard approach uses financial and non-financial information to set the company's direction and assess performance.

Further information

- Harvard Business Review: R Kaplan and D Norton, The Balanced Scorecard' (1992).
- ICSA Publishing: Non-Executive Directors Handbook, Chapter 9: Strategy (2019).

Bank accounts

Introduction

Bank accounts, and banking matters in general, are usually controlled under the authority of the board of directors of a company.

Banks have a standard form of signature mandate which will require signing by directors to identify authority for each account – this might be controlled by several directors aligned with monetary limits (e.g. payments in excess of £10,000 might require two signatures).

Signing authorities should be agreed and minuted at a formal meeting of the board of directors. The appropriate 'minute' will form part of the formal documents of the company and must be provided to the bank. In our age of electronic banking the principles remain the same, and banks require signed evidence of director approval to allow an account to operate.

NED checklist

- Has the board agreed on people and limits for the operation of the company's bank accounts? This might include checking with company executives that:
  - the appropriate 'minute' from the relevant board meeting has been approved and signed;
  - the appropriate bank mandate forms have been signed;
  - the bank has received the necessary documentation under the current UK anti-money laundering regulations; and
  - the various bank accounts and balances, along with management account reports are regularly provided (and explained) to the directors.
- Are the NEDs appropriately informed of likely cashflow requirements within the business, and therefore the suitability or otherwise of existing banking arrangements? Is their transparency on liquidity and therefore going concern viability?

Board and director evaluation

Introduction

Principle L of the UK Corporate Governance Code states:

> Annual evaluation of the board should consider its composition, diversity and how effectively members work together to achieve objectives. Individual evaluation should demonstrate whether each director continues to contribute effectively.

This principle reminds us that a board of directors is only ever a group of individuals, whose abilities and biases will evolve over time. Governance as a concept and the people empowered with governance within any organisation are not, and must not, be seen as static and fixed.

The purpose of board and director evaluation is to ensure, on a regular basis that the board and its directors continue (jointly and severally) to be effective in the oversight of the organisation.

The board evaluation is usually initiated and overseen by the chair and/ or the company secretary.

NED checklist

- What is your policy on board evaluation?
- When did the last evaluation take place and have you seen the evaluation feedback and conclusions?
- Have any (all) action points from the evaluation been addressed?
- When is the next evaluation due to take place?
- Are you required to, or should you be considering using an external evaluator?

Procedure

- Make sure you know when the annual evaluation is going to take place.

- Discuss with the chair and/or the company secretary the process and the timing of the evaluation.
- Ensure the feedback is handled in a transparent and timely manner.
- If you are using an external evaluator, make sure they understand and have an appreciation of your particular business and/or business sector. This should never just be a generic or tick-box process but must relate to the hard realities of the efficacy and effectiveness of your board, yourself and your colleagues.

Requirements

- The 2018 UK Corporate Governance Code expects all listed companies to carry out an annual evaluation.
- FTSE 350 companies are expected to use an external evaluator at least once in every three years.
- The principles and benefits of board and director evaluation are not restricted to listed companies. As a NED you need to ensure that you are part of a vibrant, balanced and diverse team of directors who are working together in the most effective manner.

Further information

- The Chartered Governance Institute: guidance note 'The board evaluation process – visual aids'. Available at: www.icsa.org.uk/knowledge/resources/board-evaluation-visual-aids
- FRC: 'Guidance on Board Effectiveness'. Available at: www.frc.org.uk/getattachment/61232f60-a338-471b-ba5a-bfed25219147/2018-Guidance-on-Board-Effectiveness-FINAL.PDF

Board balance

Introduction

The 2011 'FRC Guidance on Board Effectiveness', suggested that:

> An effective board should not necessarily be a comfortable place. Challenge, as well as teamwork, is an essential feature. Diversity in board composition is an important driver of a board's effectiveness, creating a breadth of perspective among directors, and breaking down a tendency towards group-think.

This epitomises well the need to strive towards a well-balanced board of directors.

Board diversity has become an area of high focus and there has been significant improvement in the gender balance within FTSE100 companies, but with other companies lagging behind.

Principle G of the the 2018 UK Corporate Governance Code suggests:

> The board should include an appropriate combination of executive and non-executive (and, in particular, independent non-executive) directors, such that no one individual or small group of individuals dominates the board's decision-making.

Principle K suggests:

> The board and its committees should have a combination of skills, experience and knowledge.

While it might be argued that this guidance is directed towards listed companies, in reality, all boards will benefit from striving to find an appropriate balance to match their size, sector, stakeholder expectations and commercial challenge.

NED checklist

- Is your board balanced – skills, knowledge, gender, independence, ethnicity, etc?

- If yes, would an unbiased stakeholder agree?
- If no, how can change be effected?
- Is the board sufficiently diverse to encourage independent thinking and be effective in its challenge and consideration of its agenda?
- Does the diversity and balance of the board result in healthy and challenging debate, or just group-think?
- Does each director play their part in the decision-making process?
- How would the board rate against the list of attributes in the next section?

Requirements

- The 2018 FRC Guidance on Board Effectiveness suggests that the following attributes are important within a well-balanced board of directors.
  - a source of intellect, critical assessment and judgment
  - courage
  - openness
  - honesty
  - tact
  - ability to listen
  - ability to forge relationships
  - ability to develop trust
  - strength of character.

Further information

- FRC: 'Guidance on Board Effectiveness', (2018).
- Other reviews:
  - Davies Review
  - Hampton-Alexander Review
  - Parker Review.
- ICSA Publishing: The Chartered Governance Institute Handbook on Committees, Chapter 9: Nomination Committee (2020).

Board dynamics

Introduction

A dictionary definition of the word 'dynamics' is:

> The branch of mechanics concerned with the motion of bodies under the action of forces.

This is a good definition of the practical working out of organisational governance and direction within the board room and the committee room. The psychological biases and characteristics of each person involved within a board or committee meeting are being forced to interact not just with each other but also with the micro and macro forces that have, are, and will, impact the particular organisation.

This physical interaction of these forces, the dynamics within the board and committees, will often establish the culture and wider effectiveness and viability of an organisation.

The composition of the board, its actions, and its perceived actions will set the tone for how decisions are made throughout an organisation, and how the inherent values of everyone within the organisation are worked out through everyday behaviours. This is the culture and the ethical face of the company.

These critical interactions mean that the building and governing of a balanced and effective board and organisation is challenging. The interpersonal dynamics of board members can be complex, and often rely upon trust – the trust that empowers the senior management of the organisation to achieve the strategic goals and maximise the potential from effective use of human and other resources.

Principle G of the 2018 UK Corporate Governance Code suggests that:

> The board should include an appropriate combination of executive and non-executive (and, in particular, independent non-executive) directors, such that no one individual or small group of individuals dominates the board's decision-making.

An appropriately diverse board will bring challenging dynamics but the ability to drive the optimal success from the organisation.

NED checklist

- How would you describe the dynamics of your board, and the interaction between the directors?
  - Leading or following?
  - Challenging or prosaic?
  - Participative or directed?
- How resilient are the members of the board?
- How resilient are you? As a NED, do you bring appropriate considered challenge and scepticism into the board room?
- How does your board behave? How would an informed but objective observer describe and challenge the dynamics of your board meetings?
- How would your board be aligned against the attributes mentioned in the next section?
- Did your last board evaluation include a consideration of the dynamics of the board? If not, make sure it is included in the next evaluation. (this will often need an external evaluation to bring any real and required change.)

Procedure

- The nomination committee, in close liaison with the chair, will usually take the lead on director recruitment and appointment. The replacement or appointment of directors impacts the whole board and consequently its dynamics. The nomination committee needs to give attention to the current composition and effectiveness and how a new member's skills and personal dynamics will interact and enhance the board.
- Achieving the optimal board dynamics requires consideration of the need for a diversity of personal attributes amongst board members.
- Each human being will bring different attributes. The FRC Guidance on Board Effectiveness suggest the following attributes as important for the boardroom:
  - intellect, critical assessment and judgement;
  - courage, openness and honesty;
  - tact and the ability to listen;
  - the ability to forge relationships and develop trust; and
  - strength of character and resilience.

Further information

- FRC: Guidance on Board Effectiveness (2018).
- The Chartered Governance Institute: Study Textbook, Board Dynamics (2018).
- ICSA Publishing: Board Committees Handbook, Chapter 10, 'Nomination Committee' (2020).

Borrowing powers

Introduction

Every company is deemed to have a full and open capacity to borrow money to the level at which a lender is prepared to lend, unless the articles of association (articles) place a specific restriction on the company and/or its directors.

The articles will often restrict the director's ability to exercise the full borrowing powers of the company. The limitation is usually expressed as a multiple of the company's net assets or a fixed amount of money.

Directors of any company incorporated before CA2006 require a specific authority to borrow within the articles. If the directors' capacity to borrow is not sufficient for their purposes, the articles will need to be amended by special resolution.

The board of directors may borrow by passing a resolution at the board meetings. The board may delegate its borrowing powers to a committee of directors. Such a resolution should specifically mention the aggregate amount up to which the moneys can be borrowed by the committee. The moneys borrowed, together with existing borrowings by the company, should not exceed the aggregate of the paid-up capital and reserves. A company may borrow in excess of its paid-up capital and reserves if it is agreed upon and authorised by the shareholders at a general meeting.

Where borrowing takes the form of money raised from several sources, then normally assets are charged as security for the loan payments. A register of charges identifies the assets, which are subject to the charge. There are two types of charges, namely fixed and floating charges. A charge is fixed when it covers a specific permanent or fixed asset such as land or buildings. A floating charge is a charge on the current assets of the company, which will change from time to time in the ordinary course of business.

NED checklist

- Who has the authority to approve borrowing and up to what limit?
- Is the borrowing power of the company or the directors restricted in anyway within the articles?

- If the company was incorporated before CA2006, do the articles include the right for the directors to borrow on behalf of the company?
- What is the current borrowing position of the company and, if appropriate, does this fall within the levels approved by the shareholders of the company in the articles?

Bribery Act 2010

Introduction

The Bribery Act 2010 affects all businesses in the UK. It is essential that a board of directors establish appropriate procedures to combat bribery. These will need to be aligned to the particular activity and business practices of each organisation, and be proportionate to size and risk. The Act contains four criminal offences.

- *Paying bribes*

  Offering, promising or giving a financial or other advantage with the intention of inducing a person to perform a 'relevant function or activity' 'improperly' or to reward that person for doing so.

- *Receiving bribes*

  Receiving a financial or other advantage intending that a 'relevant function or activity' should be performed 'improperly' or in an alternative manner as a result.

- *Bribery of a foreign public official*

  Offering or giving a financial or other advantage to a foreign public official with the intention of influencing, obtaining or retaining business.

- *Failure of a commercial organisation to prevent bribery*

  A commercial organisation based in or operating in the UK must be able to demonstrate that it had adequate procedures in place to prevent bribes being paid where a person associated with that organisation (including employees, agents and associated third parties) bribes another person intending to obtain or retain a business advantage.

A corporate body found guilty of one of the above offences can be subjected to an unlimited fine. An individual found guilty could face imprisonment for up to ten years, an unlimited fine or both. A business will be criminally liable if anyone associated with it pays a bribe in order to win work (in the UK or abroad).

NED checklist

- Have the implications of the Bribery Act been considered by the directors?
  - No: make sure it is on the next board agenda.
  - Yes: have we as a company taken appropriate action to protect the company and its employees from action under this Act?
- Are employees (and persons associated with the company) aware of the implications of this Act through company codes of conduct or ethics for example? How are these communicated and is training given?
- Do you regularly (annually, semi-annually) remind employees about the Act, its implications and company codes and whistleblowing procedures?
- How do you monitor the behaviour of employees in this regard, given that we might need to be able demonstrate that we have taken all reasonable to steps to prevent contravention of this Act?

Procedure

- Ensure employees are aware of their expected behaviour.
- Refresh and remind employees on regular basis (posters, intranet etc.).
- Ensure that the board review procedures on at least an annual basis.
- Ensure that there is a clear escalation procedure for any potential contravention of the varying aspects of the Act.

Requirements

The Ministry of Justice issued guidance about anti-bribery procedures in 2011. What counts as adequate will vary depending on the size of the business and the extent of the risk of bribery that it incurs (depending on the nature of its trade). The guidance suggests that because the risk of bribery is lower if business is undertaken primarily in the UK, it is unnecessary to put complex procedures in place where this is the case. It sets out six principles which it believes will help businesses to decide the extent of any procedures that they take.

- *Principle 1: Proportionate procedures*

  A commercial organisation's procedures to prevent bribery by persons associated with it are proportionate to the bribery risks it faces and to the nature, scale and complexity of the commercial organisation's activities. They are also clear, practical, accessible, effectively implemented and enforced.

- *Principle 2: Top-level commitment*

  The top-level management of a commercial organisation (be it a board of directors, the owners or any other equivalent body or person) are committed to preventing bribery by persons associated with it. They foster a culture within the organisation in which bribery is never acceptable.

- *Principle 3: Risk assessment*

  The commercial organisation assesses the nature and extent of its exposure to potential external and internal risks of bribery on its behalf by persons associated with it. The assessment is periodic, informed and documented.

- *Principle 4 – Due diligence*

  The commercial organisation applies due diligence procedures, taking a proportionate and risk-based approach, in respect of persons who perform or will perform services for or on behalf of the organisation, to mitigate identified bribery risks.

- *Principle 5 – Communication (including training)*

  The commercial organisation seeks to ensure that its bribery prevention policies and procedures are embedded and understood throughout the organisation through internal and external communication, including training, that is proportionate to the risks it faces.

- *Principle 6 – Monitoring and review*

  The commercial organisation monitors and reviews procedures designed to prevent bribery by persons associated with it and makes improvements where necessary.

Notes

- The advice to all businesses should be to have procedures well-established to monitor the activities of any of their employees, contractors or agents who may be in a position to gain work in a way that could be interpreted (however remotely) as bribery.

Further information

- Bribery Act 2010.
- ICSA Publishing: The Non-Executive Directors' Handbook (2019).
- ICSA Publishing: Non-Executive Directors' Checklist: Directors' Duties – Duty six, page 115.
- The Ministry of Justice: The Bribery Act 2010 and 2011 guidance.

Business continuity and disaster recovery

Introduction

A well-structured business continuity plan will enable a company to continue running through business interruptions of differing diverse types (e.g. IT system crash, cyber-attack, flooding, power failure, supply chain problems, the loss of key personnel, fraud, a data breach). A business continuity plan should form part of the risk management structure of an organisation.

Disaster recovery and business continuity planning will help an organisation prepare for disruptive events. In other words, anything which is likely to disrupt the normal day-to-day, week-to-week operation of the business.

Disaster recovery is a recognition of the process that is required to resume business after a major disruptive event.

Business continuity planning requires a broader approach to ensure that an organisation can continue to generate wealth following a major disruption but also after smaller, but material forces, that might impact the normal running of the organisation.

While it is impossible for a business to plan for every likely disruptive activity, a comprehensive business continuity plan will allow for how the business and its employees should react to a perceived but unlikely event (such as a total IT failure). It should also include clear guidelines on how the business and its employees should react to an unexpected event or disruption.

Ensuring that this type of planning exists is the responsibility of all directors.

NED checklist

- Does the organisation have a business continuity and disaster recovery plan? If not, why not? Has this decision been risk assessed and regularly reviewed?

- If yes, has the plan been seen, discussed and approved by the board of directors, and have the NEDs been encouraged to bring an objective perspective to the content of the plan? How often is the plan reviewed at board level?
- Are employees aware of business continuity and disaster recovery plans and, where applicable, trained on how to implement them and minimise business disruption? How often, and in what manner, is this communicated to them?
- Has the business continuity and disaster plan been tested in any manner – companies often use scenario-based situations to test such plans? When was it last tested?

Procedure

- Ensure an appropriate business continuity and disaster recovery plan exists. If not, directors should ensure that it is developed as part of the risk management strategy of the organisation.
- The board of directors should read, debate and approve the plan then ensure it is regularly reviewed.
- The plan should be communicated through the organisation as appropriate. If people are not informed, how will they know the expectations?
- Ensure that any such plan allows for two-way communication. Many potential disasters can be averted or minimised if there is a clear escalation route for an employee to bring a change in circumstances to the people with authority in an organisation.

Requirements

- The plan should allow for succession of authority in the absence of key directors or senior managers. Who is empowered to make decisions?
- Employees should receive appropriate training and there should be clarity of expectations.
- Offsite crisis meeting points should be designated.
- Alternative communication methods should be part of the plan – including how employees are informed of any disaster and when and how they should return to the workplace.
- Test the continuity plans.

Notes

- The mistakes that lead to the failure of a business continuity and disaster recovery plan:
  - inadequate planning;
  - theoretical planning without involving people at the right levels;
  - lack of substantive support and plan challenge from directors and senior managers; and
  - lack of funding for adequate and appropriate resources.

Business ethics

Introduction

The Institute of Business Ethics (IBE) suggests that:

> Business ethics is the application of ethical values to business behaviour. Business ethics is relevant both to the conduct of individuals and to the conduct of the organisation as a whole. It applies to any and all aspects of business conduct, from boardroom strategies and how companies treat their employees and suppliers to sales techniques and accounting practices. Ethics goes beyond the legal requirements for a company and is, therefore, about discretionary decisions and behaviour guided by values.

At any time within any organisation its ethics can be seen to be a combination of:

- individual and combined values of all the people involved;
- the prevailing tone of the corporate culture;
- codes of conduct that might apply across differing aspects of personal and organisational behaviour;
- societal norms and expectations;
- internal and external stakeholder expectations; and
- local, national and international law.

The perception of an organisation's ethics is closely related to its reputation. Others will judge the ethical appearance of a business alongside its other public persona, and its reputation will be created, maintained or damaged.

An organisation is only ever a group of people, and each of those people will have their own ethics, so it is good practice for an organisation to develop a 'Code of Ethics' to clearly establish and set out with clarity the expected levels of ethical behaviour that are expected from every employee.

At its best 'code of ethics' should go beyond an operational handbook and provide a stimulus for appropriate behaviour from employees toward each other and towards all stakeholders.

NED checklist

- Does the board of directors ever discuss the ethics of the organisation?
- Does the organisation have a Code of Ethics? Is it up-to-date and relevant?
- How are employees regularly reminded of the ethical expectations of the company?
- Does the board operate and behave in an ethical manner?
- Is there a clear alignment between organisational culture, organisation ethics and organisational values?
- As a NED you have the ability and experience to compare ethical approaches between organisations. How can you use this objectivity more effectively in the boardroom and in the organisation?

Requirements

- Members of The Chartered Governance Institute are expected to follow their Code of Professional Ethics and Conduct. This comprises four principles.
  - *Integrity*

    The quality of being honest and having strong moral principles. The term has been described judicially as connoting 'moral soundness, rectitude, and steady adherence to an ethical code'. It requires that members are impartial, independent and informed.
  - *High standard of service/professional competence*

    This should be delivered throughout one's working life. This involves an understanding of relevant technical, professional and business developments.
  - *Transparency*

    Members should be clear and open in their business and professional conduct.
  - *Professional behaviour*

    Members should act in a way which conforms to the relevant laws of the jurisdiction in which they are residing and/ or undertaking business transactions, and pay regard to all regulations which may have a bearing on their actions.

Further information

- Institute of Business Ethics: www.ibe.org.uk.

Business model reporting

Introduction

The provision of a business model is an expected part of the strategic report (and legal requirement for quoted companies since 2013) and should be designed to provide shareholders and stakeholders with an understanding of the company, what it does, and how and why it does it. This should align with three aspects of financial or performance metrics reporting.

- How an organisation makes money.
- How that adds stakeholder value.
- How the organisation is performing in the macro and micro economic environment within which it operates.

There are no generic business model structure expectations other than clarity, transparency and relevance.

Increasingly many organisations use an image or flow-diagram to illustrate their business model. These can be helpful when they are explained in context and irrelevant if they are just added for the sake of an image.

NED checklist

- Has the board considered the 'quick questions' listed in the Financial Reporting Lab's 2018 publication, Business Model Reporting, Risk and Viability Reporting?
  - Does your business model clearly communicate how you create value (both in terms of cash generation and non-financial value) over the longer term?
  - Is your business model disclosure comprehensive, covering all elements investors find useful that are relevant to your business, either in a single disclosure or through clear and meaningful cross referencing?
  - Does your disclosure include the business models of all your significant businesses, or refer to where that information is, and the value of combining them within one group?

- Are the key drivers of your business model(s) clear?
- Does your disclosure demonstrate how your business is unique?
- Does the business model graphic [if used] improve the understandability of the business model for those outside your organisation?

Requirements

The relevance and differing aspects of business model reporting should be guided by the underlying metrics mentioned above. Such reporting might include aspects such as the following suggestions.

- Making money:
  - Internal supply processes – what does the business do and how does it do it?
  - People and culture – company values and ethos, communication methods, alignment of employees.
  - Key drivers of the business – markets, methods and metrics.
- Adding value:
  - How, where and for whom is value added in the business model process?
  - Generation of liquidity – alignment of profitability with cash.
  - Non-financial value-add – concepts of corporate social responsibility.
  - Longer-term preservation of value – longer-term viability of the organisation.
- Performance:
  - External supply-chain process – market mix, product mix, customer balance, supplier reliability.
  - Economics of the market – comparison with trend and competitors.
  - Sustainability and viability – longevity, challenge and macro-economic forces.

Further information

- The Companies Act 2006 (Strategic Report and Directors' Report) Regulations 2013, reg. 414A.
- The Financial Reporting Lab implementation study, 'Risk and viability reporting: Where are we now?'. Available at: www.frc.org.uk/getattachment/43c07348-e175-45c4-a6e0-49f7ecabdf36/Business-Models-Lab-Implementation-Study-2018.pdf.

- Financial Reporting Lab: 'Business model reporting'. Available at: www.frc.org.uk/getattachment/4b73803d-1604-42cc-ab37-968d29f9814c/FRC-Lab-Business-model-reporting-v2.pdf.
- FRC: Guidance on the Strategic Report, 2018.
- ICSA Publishing: Non-Executive Directors' Handbook, Chapter 9, 2019.

Business names

Introduction

A business name is a name or title by which a company may trade other than its corporate or registered name. Companies House no longer maintain a register of business names.

All official communications, including business stationery, issued by a company using a business name must show the company's registered name in full as well as the business name being used, in addition to the other statutory requirements.

Any company using a business name must ensure that it does not infringe upon other registered names or trademarks. Likewise, such a company must not pass itself off as another registered company, partnership or sole trader.

NED checklist

- Does the company have any business name(s) that it uses as an alternative to its corporate or registered name?
- If a business name is used, do all business communications contain the required corporate identity, including the registered name in addition to the business name?
- Is the company's registered name displayed at all business premises using the business name?

Notes

- A company that has been dormant from the date of its incorporation does not need to have its name displayed at its registered office.

Cadbury Code

Introduction

Upheavals in the UK financial markets in the late 1980s were epitomised by the problems surrounding Bank of Credit and Commerce International, Polly Peck, Trinity Mirror and Robert Maxwell, and a growing controversy over directors' remuneration. The UK Government of the time commissioned a committee, chaired by Adrian Cadbury, to consider the behaviour of companies and their directors within harsh and challenging economic climates.

The resultant report entitled The Financial Aspects of Corporate Governance was published in 1992 and frequently referred to as the Cadbury Code. It became the foundation for all UK corporate governance initiatives. Many of its principles still sit at the centre of the UK Corporate Governance Code and the associated governance behaviour that is rightly expected from directors.

NED checklist

- How well does our company align with the original Cadbury Code Principles?
- The areas covered in the Cadbury Code are:
  - board effectiveness
  - the chair
  - non-executive directors
  - professional advice
  - directors' training
  - board structures and procedures
  - the company secretary
  - directors' responsibilities
  - standards of conduct
  - nomination committees

- internal controls
- audit committees
- internal audit
- board remuneration
- financial reports
- reporting practice
- pensions governance
- auditing
- shareholders.

Requirement

- There is no direct requirement today resulting from the 1992 report, other than its ethos permeating throughout UK corporate governance.
- It is still worthwhile for directors to read this 1992 report and to consider how little has changed in the need for effective governance, and how many of the straightforward clauses of the relatively short and succinct Cadbury Code are equally applicable to today's directors and boards.

Notes

- The title of the Cadbury Code – The Financial Aspects of Corporate Governance – underpins that corporate governance must always be more than just a 'tick-box' process. The manner in which an organisation establishes it corporate governance will have a direct or indirect effect on its financial viability.

Further information

- The original 1992 Cadbury Report is available at: www.icaew.com/-/media/corporate/files/library/subjects/corporate-governance/financial-aspects-of-corporate-governance.ashx?la=en.

Capability and competence

Introduction

Driving the success of an organisation is a core duty and accountability of the directors.

In a cyclical manner, this process will start with effective strategic planning, objective setting and ensuring that the appropriate resources are in place to enable the delivery of those objectives.

People will always be a significant part of the resource structure of every organisation.

Directors must therefore ensure that the human resource within the organisation has the appropriate levels of capability and competence.

- A capability is the potential to achieve an outcome.
- A competence is the ability to apply and utilise a capability.

The larger the organisation, the more remote the directors will be from an awareness of the selection, capabilities and competences of the people employed. However, as it is these people who will either succeed or fail in the delivery of the strategic objectives, directors must establish and monitor a human resource strategy to align with the wider strategic objectives of the organisation.

NED checklist

- Is there a clear and transparent human resources strategy?
- Does the board ever consider whether the organisation has an optimal mixture of capability and competence?
- Does the board ever consider if there is an optimal mixture of capability and competence around the board table?
- Do you use your independence as a NED to meet people fulfilling different roles across the organisation, and therefore make your own assessment of capability and competence? Do you feed this back to the board as a whole?
- Does the board understand the core capabilities and competences required at all levels within the organisation? Where are the gaps?

Chair and CEO role separation

Introduction

Provision 9 of the UK Corporate Governance Code 2018 states:

> The roles of Chair and Chief Executive should not be exercised by the same individual. A Chief Executive should not become Chair of the same company. If, exceptionally, this is proposed by the board, major shareholders should be consulted ahead of appointment.

This separation of the roles of chair and chief executive officer (CEO) has been one of the central tenets of perceived governance effectiveness since the Cadbury Code of 1992 and is seen as an important safeguard of shareholder interests.

A frequently used maxim is 'the chair runs the board, but the CEO runs the business'.

NED checklist

- Is there a clear distinction between the roles of chair and CEO?
- Is there a written record of their individual duties and of areas where they are required and expected to work closely together?
- Is there a healthy and constructive relationship between the chair and the CEO?
- Is the relationship too close and therefore inhibits debate and challenge?
- Is there a disconnect such that political meandering is required in the boardroom?
- Was the working relationship between chair and CEO explored during the last board evaluation?
- Does the chair interfere or appear to interfere in the operational running and oversight of the business?

Procedure

- Ensure a clear written distinction exists between the roles of chair and CEO.

Requirements

- Companies required to comply with the UK Corporate Governance Code will need to ensure either that they have strong shareholder support if they decide either that the roles of chair and CEO can be combined, or that the CEO is the natural successor the chair.
- Provision 14 of the UK Corporate Governance Code 2018 states:

  'The responsibilities of the chair, chief executive, senior independent director, board and committees should be clear, set out in writing, agreed by the board and made publicly available'.

Further information

- FRC: UK Corporate Governance Code (2018).
- FRC: 'Guidance on Board Effectiveness', (2018).

Committee terms of reference

Introduction

In every organisation there will be a range of committees. Some committees will be formally constituted committees of the board, and so derive their authority from the board of directors. Other committees will inevitably exist across an organisation, often for generic and ongoing activities and requirements (e.g. health and safety committee) but sometimes for one-off specific projects (e.g. the implementation of a new IT system).

In every case it is advisable and important to ensure that a committee has clear and concise terms of reference (ToR).

As a NED your primary interest will be the main three committees of the board – usually nomination, remuneration and audit. If risk is not covered within the remit of the audit committee, then there is often a board risk committee, which can also be constituted as a board committee – not to be confused with a risk management committee of the company, which is often led by the CEO.

The point of the ToR for any committee is to ensure a two-directional clarity – where does authority derive from, and for what purposes is it to be used?

As a NED, you will play a part in the formulation and review of the ToR for board committees, but it is also important to be aware of the wider committee structure within an organisation to understand the culture of debate and decision making that exists.

NED checklist

- What committees has the board decided to create? How many members and what type of members are required on each committee? Are the recommendations under the UK Corporate Governance Code (or similar Code) followed?
- What are committees' parameters as per the ToR?
- Are the roles and responsibilities of each committee clear and understood by all members?

- How and when do the committees report back on its deliberations and findings?

Procedure

- The ToR should identify how a chair is appointed for the committee. This may be an appointment made by those to whom the committee is accountable, or it may be an appointment made by the members of the committee themselves from within the appointed members of that committee.
- The ToR should identify the operating and reporting requirements of the committee.
- The ToR should identify how and when members of the committee are appointed and removed.

Requirements

- On initial appointment as a NED, and subsequently, ensure you are aware of the committees where you are expected to serve. Obtain a copy of the relevant ToR, ensure that it is clear, and that you understand the remit and the requirement. Be ready to challenge if you feel the ToR are either unclear or inappropriate for the expectations.
- Ensure there is a clarity of committee structure within the organisation and that the various ToRs are designed to deliver an upward flow of assurance from 'operational' committees, through 'review' committees to board committees.
- A useful area to test the veracity of committee ToR is how risk is identified, assessed, challenged, mitigated and reported through the various committees (and their ToR) within an organisation. Eventually 'information' will reach the board through either the audit committee or the risk committee, but the originating data will have passed through different layers of committee (formal and informal) within the organisation. An awareness of this can enhance and inform the NED role in terms of organisational understanding and assurance.

Notes

- Check, usually through the company secretary, that a 'map' exists of committees that operate within the organisation. Ask to see the various ToR: their availability (or otherwise) will provide a useful information base for further consideration.

Further information

- FRC: UK Corporate Governance Code (2018).
- ICSA Publishing: The Non-Executive Directors' Handbook (2019).
- The Chartered Governance Institute: guidance note, Terms of reference for committees'.

Companies House

Introduction

Companies House is the UK's registrar of companies and is an executive agency and trading fund of Her Majesty's Government. It operates under the remit of the Department for Business, Energy and Industrial Strategy (BEIS) and is a member of the Public Data Group.

All forms of company are incorporated and registered with Companies House as required by CA2006.

All registered limited companies, including subsidiary, small and dormant companies must file annual financial statements with Companies House in addition to the required annual company return.

NED checklist

- Review the Companies House record for your company and/or for other companies with which you may have a material or financial connection.
- Upon appointment as a director, and also when leaving a company, ensure that your details are held correctly at Companies House for each and every directorship.
- Ensure that all required annual returns are submitted correctly and on time. As an officer of the company, you have equal responsibility with all other officers for ensuring that this happens. In particular this is the annual filing of the accounts of the company, and the annual return (confirmation statement).
- Companies can be found on the Companies House website through use of either their trading name or their registered number.
- The following information can be downloaded free of charge for any company:
  - registered address and date of incorporation;
  - current and resigned officers;
  - document images;

- mortgage charge data;
- previous company names;
- insolvency information; and
- latest company filings – accounts, changes of director, other changes to the status or share structure of the company.

- It is also possible to set up an email alert for any changes to the details of a company.

Notes

- Almost all company filing is now completed online.
- Questions on general or specific matters should be directed to the appropriate Companies House site, dependent upon location of the registered office of the company:

England and Wales
Companies House
Crown Way
Maindy
Cardiff CF14 3UZ
DX 33050 Cardiff 1

Contact Centre: +44 (0)303 1234 500
Website: www.companieshouse.gov.uk
Email: enquiries@companieshouse.gov.uk

London Information Centre
4 Abbey Orchard Street
Westminster
London SW1P 2HT
Contact Centre: +44 (0)303 1234 500

Scotland
Companies House
4th Floor, Edinburgh Quay 2
139 Fountainbridge
Edinburgh EH3 9FF
Contact Centre: +44 (0)303 1234 500

Northern Ireland
Companies House
2nd Floor, The Linenhall
32–38 Linenhall Street
Belfast BT2 8BG
Contact Centre: +44 (0)303 1234 500

Companies House filing

Introduction

Companies House is the United Kingdom's registrar of companies and is an executive agency and trading fund of Her Majesty's Government. It operates under the remit of the Department for Business, Energy and Industrial Strategy (BEIS) and is a member of the Public Data Group.

All forms of company are incorporated and registered with Companies House as required by CA2006.

There are a number of regular returns which must be sent to Companies House. It is the duty of all directors and officers of a company to ensure that all such returns are filed accurately, on time, and (if necessary) with the appropriate fee.

NED checklist

- Be clear as to who in the company takes the lead and the ownership of submitting all required returns to Companies House.
- Periodically, as appropriate, check that such returns are being sent, and that no regular returns are outstanding – this can be carried out through a quick search on your company on the Companies House website.
- It is good practice for directors to be advised by the company secretary or whoever has the submission responsibility, as and when key returns are submitted.
- Key returns to be aware of:
  - annual confirmation statement (formerly known as the annual return);
  - submission of annual accounts;
  - appointment or resignation of a director;
  - any change in registered office or SAIL address;
  - any change to the articles of association; and
  - resolutions or agreements agreed by the members of a company.

Company secretary

Introduction

The Companies Act 2006 requires a public limited company to appoint a suitably qualified individual to the role of company secretary.

Private companies need not appoint or retain a company secretary but may do so if they wish. If a private company appoints a company secretary then that person fulfils the same role and has the same level of accountability and statutory requirement as if they had been appointed by a public limited company.

If a company secretary is not appointed then the directors and any other officers of the company are equally accountable for ensuring that all statutory obligations are met.

The company secretary is generally a key member of the executive team who is appointed by the board as an officer of the company. They have specific responsibility for advising the board through the chair on all governance matters and for ensuring good information flows within the board and its committees and between senior management and non-executive directors, as well as facilitating induction and assisting with professional development.

The UK Corporate Governance Code states that the appointment and removal of the company secretary is a matter for the board as a whole. The company secretary is responsible to the board of directors collectively rather than to any individual director.

The company secretary will need to have knowledge of the legal, regulatory and administrative framework in which the organisation operates. This will vary from a premium listed public limited company with thousands of shareholders, to a private limited company, a charity or a service provider in the public sector.

Any individual appointed as a company secretary should have the experience and/or ability to understand and fulfil the breadth of requirement of the role.

NED checklist

- Does the company have a company secretary? Have they been appointed correctly in accordance with the constitution and, if a public company, do they meet the company secretary requirements of CA2006?
- What are the reporting lines of the company secretary? This is often important for understanding the culture and the board dynamics within an organisation.
- If working in a private company and there is no company secretary, is it clear who takes the lead in ensuring that all statutory obligations are being met?
- Does the company secretary ensure that all meeting paperwork – agenda, minutes, reports etc. – are circulated in due time to allow consideration ahead of meetings?

Further information

- ICSA publishing: Company Secretary's Handbook (2019).
- ICSA publishing: Company Secretary's Checklists (2019).

Company size criteria

Introduction

The Companies Act 2006, as amended and updated from time to time, places limited companies into different size categories. The company size determines the level and detail of reporting that is required from a company. It also determines whether an audit is required and enables members to simplify certain procedures.

- A company classed as a **micro entity** must meet at least two of the following criteria:
  - turnover must not be more than £632,000;
  - the balance sheet total must not be more than £316,000; and
  - the average number of employees must not be more than 10.
- A **small private company** must meet at least two of the following criteria:
  - turnover must not be more than £10.2 million;
  - the balance sheet total must not be more than £5.1 million; and
  - the average number of employees must not be more than 50.
- A **medium-sized private company** must meet at least two of the following criteria
  - turnover must not be more than £36 million;
  - the balance sheet total must not be more than £18 million; and
  - the average number of employees must not be more than 250.
- A **large private company** must therefore meet at least two of the following criteria:
  - turnover must be more than £36 million;
  - the balance sheet total must be more than £18 million; and
  - the average number of employees must be more than 250.
- A **large private company** for the purpose of the Wates Principles must meet either or both of the following criteria:

- more than 2,000 employees; and
- a turnover of more than £200 million and a balance sheet total of more than £2 billion.

NED checklist

- Verify the company's size criteria and associated reporting requirements with the company executive responsible.

Compensation for loss of office

Introduction

The terms of engagement and/or director's service contract for each individual executive director should include details of notice periods required and expected from either the director or the company to terminate the agreement. This should also include normal arrangements for any compensation that will or may be paid as a result of loss of office.

NED checklist

- Ensure the service contract is clear and explicit concerning:
  - termination of agreement by the director;
  - termination of the agreement by the company;
  - anticipated compensation that may be paid and its dependent circumstances; and
  - the need for shareholder agreement or otherwise.
- Determine whether there has been any history in the company of the payment of compensation to a director for loss of office.
- Be clear of the trigger points for potential loss of office.
- Clarify whether all directors of the company are engaged on identical terms.
- Have all remuneration reporting requirements been met with regard to any director who has left the company?

Procedure

- A director's service contract can be ended for a number for reasons with different potential immediate outcomes in the relationship between director and company.
- Summary dismissal for gross misconduct – the director would leave with immediate effect, but there is a need for clear evidence from the company to support such an action.

- Terminate contract and require director to work a notice period – this will usually deliver a detrimental outcome for the company with a director being demotivated.
- Terminate contract and put director on garden leave – this will limit the threats of any competition threatening the business if the director moves to a rival. Terms of such an arrangement need to be deemed reasonable to the director if subsequently challenged in a court or tribunal.
- Terminate the contract instantly with a payment in lieu of any notice – this provides a rapid solution with no breach of contract risk.
- Initiate a dialogue and negotiate a compensation package – this can work well if the director and company have a good relationship and the reasons for departure are understood and not acrimonious. There remain legal risks if the director then decides to pursue an unfair dismissal claim.

Requirements

- Sections 215 to 222 of CA2006 require shareholder agreement to payment to a director for loss of office. However, s. 220(10) removes this shareholder expectation where a payment is made in good faith:
  - in discharge of an existing legal obligation;
  - by way of damages for a breach of such obligation;
  - by way of settlement or compromise of any claim arising in connection with the termination of a person's office or employment; and
  - by way of pensions in respect of past services.
- Principle 39 of the 2018 UK Corporate Governance Code suggests:

  > The remuneration committee should ensure compensation commitment in directors' terms of appointment do not reward poor performance. They should be robust in reducing compensation to reflect departing directors' obligations to mitigate loss.

- Section 144 of the 2018 FRC Guidance on Board Effectiveness states:

  > Compensation commitments due to directors under their terms of appointment in the event of loss of office should be proportionate and variable by discretion, so that the remuneration committee can vary compensation where appropriate to the circumstances and to reflect departing directors' conduct and performance.

Further information

- The Companies Act 2006.
- FRC: UK Corporate Governance Code (2018).
- FRC: 'Guidance on Board Effectiveness', (2018).

Comply or explain

Introduction

The concept of 'comply or explain' sits at the centre of the UK approach to corporate governance. It has underpinned UK governance expectations since the original Cadbury Code of 1992 (the Financial Aspects of Corporate Governance) and is the basis of the flexible approach that exists within UK governance.

The Code is not designed to be a rigid set of rules, but is a set of principles (18 in the 2018 Code) to guide the underpinning governance ethos and expectations, supported by provisions (41 in the 2018 Code). These, in turn, provide the benchmark for how directors might report on their compliance with the principles. Where a company is unable to 'comply' with these provisions, it should 'explain' and justify the reasons for not doing so.

The 'comply or explain' approach recognises that each company or organisation is different, that the generic Code principles and provisions might not be directly applicable to all circumstances, and that effective governance can often be achieved by other means.

A condition of UK Listing Rules (rule LR 9.8.6) is that if a company chooses to deviate from the Code it should carefully explain the reasons to its shareholders, recognising that their voting intentions might be influenced as a result.

Many 'non-listed' companies and organisations choose to follow the UK Code, its principles and provisions as part of their approach to governance. Although not required to strictly follow a 'comply or explain' approach, such organisations usually use the rigour of such an approach to bring external and internal assurance to their governance.

NED checklist

- Are the shares of your company listed and traded on the London Stock Exchange?

- Yes:
  - It is important to consider how the principles and provisions of the UK Code are interpreted and complied with.
  - If the company is not fully compliant, it is important that you, as a director, are satisfied with the explanation(s) given in the latest annual report and accounts.
- No:
  - If your company states that it fulfils its governance requirement (e.g. as required by companies with shares traded on the Alternative Investment Market (AIM) and/or companies falling under the Wates Large Private Company parameters) is it complying in full or only partially, and are any explanations robust and appropriate?

Procedure

- If your company or organisation is required to or chooses to follow the UK Code, ensure that you are familiar with the UK Code, its principles and provisions.
- If your company or organisation is not required to and chooses not to follow the UK Code, you should still ensure that you are aware of the UK Code, its principles and provisions to consider whether your governance could be enhanced and/or strengthened through voluntary compliance.

Requirements

- Although compliance with the UK Code is voluntary, the UK Listing Rules (rule LR 9.8.6) require listed companies to disclose, in their annual report and accounts, that the company has:
  - applied the principles of the UK Corporate Governance Code;
  - complied with all relevant provisions of the Code; or
  - if it has not complied with all provisions, it has provided an explanation of which provisions were not complied with and the reasons for non-compliance.

Notes

- The underlying concept of 'comply or explain' can act as a useful challenge and benchmark for many other aspects of corporate life. As a NED it is important to understand the generic, specific and sectoral stakeholder expectations of your organisation, and to be able to challenge how, when, where and why you do or not comply with such expectations.

Further information

- FRC: UK Corporate Governance Code (2018).
- AIM Rules 26.
- Quoted Companies Alliance (QCA): Corporate Governance Code for small and mid-sized companies (2018).
- ICSA Publishing: The Non-Executive Directors' Handbook, Chapter 1 (2019).

Control principles

Introduction

Control forms a key part of the governance oversight role of a director and should be enhanced around the board table by the independent challenge from the NEDs. They will not usually have been involved in establishing the systems and processes where the control measures are required, nor in the design of that control. They should therefore be better placed to bring an objective and unbiased challenge on effectiveness and efficiency of control.

Control sits as part of the threefold requirements at the centre of a director's governance role.

- The directors will establish a strategy which sets the direction of the organisation into a perceived, but uncertain future.
- That uncertainty will bring risks – some perceived and some not.
- Those directors need to be assured that appropriate control measures have been established to identify, control and mitigate the risks that will occur while delivering the strategic objectives of the organisation.

This is best summarised in Principle O of the 2018 UK Corporate Governance Code, which states:

> The board should establish procedures to manage risk, oversee the internal control framework, and determine the nature and extent of the principal risks the company is willing to take to achieve its long-term strategic objectives.

Principle C also states that

> The board should also establish a framework of prudent and effective controls, which enable risk to be assessed and managed.

Under the Code provisions, the audit committee is responsible for

> reviewing the company's internal financial controls and internal control and risk management systems, unless expressly addressed by a separate board risk committee composed of independent non-executive directors, or by the board itself (Provision 25).

Furthermore, the

> board should monitor the company's risk management and internal control systems and, at least annually, carry out a review of their effectiveness and report on that review in the annual report. The monitoring and review should cover all material controls, including financial, operational and compliance controls' (Provision 29).

Further guidance on the implementation of the Code principles and provisions can be found in the FRC guidance listed below.

Even where companies are not subject to the UK Corporate Governance Code, the above principles remain sound guidance and should be considered and regularly reviewed by all boards as part of their governance discussions.

NED checklist

- Even if your company is not subject to the Code, is control and the principles and provisions of the Code a regular part of the board agenda? If not, then why not?
- Do the control measures align with the risks that derive from delivering the strategic objectives of the organisation?
- Are there clear owners of control procedures who give confidence to the NEDs?
- How objective are the control systems? Are they just controlled within the operational structure with minimal summarised reporting to NEDs, or do you have an appropriate level of clarity as to the nature and robustness of control?
- When were the control measures last tested, challenged and reviewed? How were the results reported to the board and discussed?
- When did you, as a NED, bring an independent perspective or challenge to the internal control oversight review?

Procedure

- Ensure that the strategic direction and the strategic objectives of the organisation are clear and transparent at board level and within the business (as appropriate).
- Align the perceived risks with the strategic objectives.
- Enable the business to develop appropriate control measures.
- Require transparent reporting such that directors are assured that optimal control exists at an appropriate level of granularity within the operational flow.

Notes

- Control is required to deal with both anticipated and emergent risks. There are four logical levers of control.
  - *Analysis* – the identification and understanding of the risk, determining how it should be controlled, initiating that control.
  - *Audit* – oversight, review, challenge and reporting of the controls that have been implemented as a result of the analysis.
  - *Assessment* – an objective consideration of the appropriateness and robustness of the control measures based on the analysis and audit stages.
  - *Assurance* – the confidence by directors that they can deliver assurance to shareholders and stakeholders based on the analysis, audit and assessment stages.

Further information

- ICSA Publishing: The Non-Executive Directors' Handbook, Chapter 10 (2019).
- FRC: UK Corporate Governance Code (2018).
- FRC: 'Guidance on Risk Management, Internal Control and Related Financial and Business Reporting', (2014).
- FRC: 'Guidance on Going Concern Basis of Accounting and Reporting on Solvency and Liquidity Risks', (2016).

Corporate disclosure

Introduction

An accepted principle of establishing a limited liability company is that the directors and officers will have a duty to provide regular disclosure to shareholders and stakeholders.

In essence, such disclosure is the act of releasing all relevant information which may influence or impact upon an investment or other risk-based decision.

Disclosures may be statutory, as required by CA2006; regulatory, as required by the Disclosure and Transparency Regulations (DTR) and Listing Rules for a listed company, or by some other organisational or sectoral structure; best practice, as outlined in the UK Corporate Governance Code; or voluntary, as deemed appropriate from time-to-time by an organisation.

Directors and officers of a company are held liable by CA2006 for all statutory required disclosure and also usually for all other required disclosure. The reporting requirements under CA2006 s. 172 provide for an enhanced statutory reporting disclosure for all except small and medium-sized companies.

NED checklist

- Be aware of the status, size and nature of your company or organisation. This will enable you to determine the different levels of disclosure required.
- Be clear who in the company is responsible for delivering disclosure to the appropriate authority in a timely and accurate manner.
- Does the board have a past and future timeline record of all such disclosures?
- Do you have confidence in the manner in which corporate disclosure is handled in your company?

Requirements

- Companies House requirements:
  - annual confirmation statement;
  - appointment of a director or secretary;
  - termination of appointment of a director or secretary;
  - change of particulars of a director or secretary;
  - change in situation of registered office and/or SAIL address;
  - allotment of shares;
  - change in accounting reference date; and
  - annual report and accounts, or dormant company accounts.
- Information to be available at registered office or SAIL address – variously available for inspection under the restrictions of CA2006:
  - register of members;
  - register of charges and instruments creating charges;
  - register of directors (and secretaries if appropriate);
  - directors' service contracts;
  - persons with significant control (PSC) register;
  - records of resolution, minutes of company and directors' meetings;
  - contracts relating to purchase of own shares;
  - register of debenture holders; and
  - register of interest in shares.
- Corporate disclosures under the DTR and Listing Rules for UK companies listed on the London Stock Exchange (AIM companies have similar requirements):
  - any information on new developments which could lead to a substantial movement in the share price;
  - any change in the company's expected performance which is materially different from the expectation of the market (e.g. a profit warning);
  - alterations to capital.
  - changes in class rights;
  - any major acquisitions or disposals;
  - the announcement of full and half-year results;
  - purchase of own shares or redemption of securities;

- information relating to major shareholders where they control major voting rights;
- the outcome of any decisions made by shareholders in general meeting;
- any substantial change in the way the company is managed (e.g. a change in the accounting reference date);
- the board's decisions on dividends;
- any change in directors, including their areas of responsibility;
- in respect of a person discharging managerial responsibility, any change in their interest in the shares or debentures of the company, including any options granted to or exercised by them under an employee share scheme; and
- the issue of the company's statutory accounts and their interest half year report.

Further information

- ICSA Publishing: The Non-Executive Directors' Handbook, chapter 13 (2019).

Corporate governance

Introduction

The UK Corporate Governance Code 2018 quotes the definition of corporate governance provided in the report of the Cadbury Committee (1992): 'Corporate governance is the system by which companies are directed and controlled.'

Corporate governance is a conceptual process of oversight and accountability that needs to be undertaken at a practical level by those appointed to the role by the owners (shareholders) and sometimes other stakeholders of an organisation. Under the law, a NED has the same level of accountability as all other directors, but with the particular expectation of an external (and often independent) perspective of challenge and objectivity.

The word governance has its origins in the Greek word *kubernao* which means 'to steer'. It was used by Plato in a metaphorical sense to describe the steering or guiding of the state. This is a good analogy for those empowered with governance responsibilities.

Effective corporate governance can be defined as the assurance that a governance structure exists within an organisation which is appropriate for it, as an organisation, at this moment in its evolution and for the foreseeable future, within the expectations of its stakeholders.

Since the Cadbury Code in 1992, there has been an increased focus on corporate governance. In many organisations it is taken for granted, and perceived as being effective – until the point where something goes wrong, then the judgement of the directors is often called into question (historic examples include Maxwell and Polly Peck, more recent examples include Carillion and Patisserie Valerie).

NED checklist

- Make sure you understand the governance requirement for your organisation:
  - What type of company or organisation are you?
  - Do you have to follow a particular code of practice?

- ▷ Who has set the governance principles and governance culture of the organisation?
- ▷ Is governance taken seriously; if not, why not?

- Consider the current governance systems and the mixture of directors, within the context of the shareholder and stakeholder expectation (cross-refer to CA2006 s. 172 requirements) and the recent past history of the organisation (refer to previous governance statements, board minutes, internal policies etc.).

Requirements

- Companies whose shares are listed and traded on the London Stock Exchange are expected to comply with the UK Corporate Governance Code (issued by the FRC); if they choose not to comply with any of the principles of provisions of the Code, they are expected to explain their rationale in their annual report and accounts.
- Companies whose shares are listed and traded on the Alternative Investment Market (AIM) are required to either follow the UK Corporate Governance Code or another recognised code of their choosing (such as that provided by the Quoted Companies Alliance) and state their choice and approach to governance within their annual report and accounts.
- Companies who are classed within an upper tier of large private companies (a company that satisfies either or both of the following criteria: more than 2,000 employees; or a turnover of more than £200 million with a balance sheet of more than £2 billion) are required to follow the Wates principles on corporate governance.
- All other private companies will undertake corporate governance as a natural part of their day-to-day oversight but are not generally required to follow a particular code of practice; however, drawing from the any of the existing codes listed above is beneficial.
- Many private companies and other organisations are expected to comply with or follow a governance code of practice that might have been issued by their regulator or by another sectoral oversight body (e.g. Foundation Trust hospitals are expected to follow the Monitor Code of Governance; the Association of Financial Mutuals issued a Code of Governance for their members in January 2019).

Procedure

- Assess the governance culture of your organisation from an objective position, what does it look like to key stakeholders?
- If your organisation is required to follow the UK Code or another Code, ensure you are familiar with that Code and have considered how your organisation does or does not follow the expectations.

- Consider how your organisational reputation is or could be linked to the manner in which you, as a NED, and your organisation are exercising corporate governance.

Notes

- Most organisations in the UK operate under a 'unitary' board structure – one board of directors (an appropriate mixture of EDs and NEDs) are appointed by the members in accordance with the constitution of the organisation. However, CA2006 presumes that each director has an equal level of accountability, irrespective of whether they are an ED, NED, de facto director, or a shadow director. Each director therefore needs to take personal responsibility for their own personal compliance with all governance expectations.

Further information

- FRC: UK Corporate Governance Code (2018).
- The Wates Corporate Governance Principles for Large Private Companies (2018).
- QCA Corporate Governance Code (2018).
- ICSA Publishing: The Non-Executive Directors' Handbook, chapter 1 (2019).

Corporate Manslaughter Act 2007

Introduction

The Corporate Manslaughter and Corporate Homicide Act 2007 introduced a new offence of corporate manslaughter in England, Wales and Northern Ireland, and corporate homicide in Scotland. Before 2007, an organisation could only be convicted of manslaughter if a significantly senior employee of the organisation had committed the offence and was seen as embodying the mind of the organisation.

An indictable offence is committed if the way in which the organisation's activities are managed or organised causes a person's death and amounts to a gross breach of a relevant duty of care owed by the organisation to the deceased person.

The way in which the activities of the organisation are managed or organised by its directors and senior management is seen as a substantial element in the committing of any such offence under the Act.

An organisation, and therefore its directors and senior management, owes a duty of care, under the law of negligence, to its employees and other stakeholders involved in working with and alongside the organisation, its products and services.

A breach of that duty of care by the organisation occurs when it can be shown that the duty fell far below what could reasonably be expected of the organisation in a particular set of circumstances.

The Health and Safety Executive will decide, after appropriate investigation, whether there is sufficient evidence that the directors and senior management have been negligent to the point where a corporate manslaughter action might be appropriate. If an individual director or senior manager is also found liable for the offence of manslaughter they are likely to be prosecuted under the Health and Safety at Work etc Act 1974.

The Act allows for an unlimited fine to be levied on an organisation found guilty of corporate manslaughter. It further recommends that a fine is based on the size and turnover of the organisation with a starting fine of £300,000. Several fines levied under this legislation have been in excess of £1 million. The Act also can require a convicted organisation to publish details of its conviction and fine.

NED checklist

- Have the implications of the Corporate Manslaughter Act been considered by the directors?
  - No: Make sure it is on the next board agenda.
  - Yes: Have you, as a company, taken appropriate action to protect the company and its employees from action under this Act?
- Are employees aware of the implications of this Act? How? Do you regularly (annually, semi-annually) remind people about the Act and its implications?
- Is the associated behaviour included in your Code of Ethics?
- How do you monitor the behaviour of your employees in this regard? As directors, you need to be able to demonstrate that you have taken all reasonable steps to prevent contravention of this Act.
- In the case of a serious incident, who will lead the company's external communication with media and other interested parties?

Procedure

- Ensure that there is a clear internal health and safety policy with regards to the protection of all employees.
- Ensure that all employees receive training and regular reminders of their duty of care to their colleagues.
- Ensure that all and every health and safety incident within the organisation is treated with an appropriate duty of care, and is investigated, recorded and reported as appropriate.
- Ensure that the directors receive a regular report regarding health and safety incidents within the organisation, under that any major incident is escalated to the board of directors at the earliest opportunity – not necessarily waiting for the next board meeting to take place.

Further information

- Crown Prosecution Service (CPS): Guidance on Corporate Manslaughter. Available at: www.cps.gov.uk/legal-guidance/corporate-manslaughter.

Corporate social responsibility

Introduction

Corporate social responsibility (CSR) is aligned with a range of differing aspects of the life of an organisation.

- The impact that organisational decisions have on the world, its environment and its people.
- The ethical norms and behaviour that can or cannot be expected from any organisation, and then, at a deeper level, the behaviours that can be rightly expected from any particular organisation, within its own sector and context.
- The manner in which employees of the organisation are treated.
- The ethics and ethos which are expected throughout the organisation:
  - ethics being the behavioural traits that are visible; and
  - ethos being the ethical stance being taken by those structure and oversee the culture within an organisation.

Recognition of CSR by an organisation is a commitment to contribute to economic development from within an ethical framework, while seeking to improve the quality of life for its employees and their families, the local community and society at large.

Section 172 of CA2006 requires the directors of all UK limited companies, as a duty, to ensure that their decision making encompasses the wider stakeholder environment. Although not referred to as CSR, the link is clear. Corporate reporting requirements, enhanced in early 2019, require the annual report, of all companies except small companies, to describe how the directors of the company have fulfilled their obligation under this duty.

Directors are required to behave with a wider stakeholder and CSR awareness and are required to explain and illustrate how they have done so.

NED checklist

- Does the company have a defined and clear approach to, and policies regarding CSR?
- Are CSR policies and reporting aligned with the strategy of the company and the various regulatory and other reporting requirements?
- Are the NEDs involved in the formulation and/or challenge of the CSR dimension of the corporate strategy and culture?
- Do the NEDs have the opportunity to comment upon and challenge the CSR policies, oversight and reporting produced by the company?
- Are the NEDs encouraged to bring a challenging and more objective approach to CSR within the company based upon their ongoing external experience?
- Have directors considered the potential reputational damage to the organisation through an actual or perceived laissez-faire approach to CSR?

Procedure

- When evolving the CSR approach of the organisation, directors should ensure that the following aspects are considered, as a minimum:
  - Internal
    - employee policies concerning welfare, health and safety, working conditions etc;
    - job design, training and communication;
    - employee pay and benefits; and
    - legal requirements in relation to staff welfare, rights etc
  - External
    - impact upon the environment;
    - safety and impact of products and services;
    - markets and marketing initiatives;
    - handling of suppliers, and insight into supplier's suppliers (beware of Modern Slavery dimensions) (see the checklist on the 'Modern Slavery Act 2015' on page 199);
    - employment rights and minimum wage expectations;
    - community activities; and
    - human rights implications of the business model.

Requirements

- Directors of a company classed as large under CA2006 are required to include a s. 172 report as part of the strategic report. This requires commentary as to how the directors have addressed their stakeholder responsibilities, including commentary on the impact of the company's operations on the community and the environment.
- Directors of a listed company have enhanced reporting requirements including carbon and greenhouse gas emissions.
- The UK Government Green Finance Strategy established a Task Force on Climate-related Financial Disclosures (TCFD). Under this initiative the UK Government expects all listed companies and large asset owners to be disclosing in line with the TCFD recommendations by 2022. These are:
  - the organisation's governance around climate-related risks and opportunities;
  - the actual and potential impacts of climate related risks and opportunities on the organisation's business, strategy, and financial planning;
  - process is used by the organisation to identify, assess, and manage climate related risks; and
  - the metrics and targets used to assess and manage relevant climate related risks and opportunities.

Further information

- UK Government: Green Finance Report. Available at: assets.publishing.service.gov.uk/government/uploads/system/uploads/attachment_data/file/820284/190716_BEIS_Green_Finance_Strategy_Accessible_Final.pdf
- ICSA Publishing: The Non-Executive Directors' Handbook, chapter 13 (2019).

Culture

Introduction

In the introduction to the 2018 UK Corporate Governance Code, the FRC suggests:

> a company's culture should promote integrity and openness, value diversity and be responsive to the views of shareholders and wider stakeholders.

The dictionary defines culture as:

- the arts and other expressions of human intellectual achievement; and
- the ideas, customs and common social behaviour of a particular people or society.

These definitions suggest that the concept of culture must be broad enough to cover tangible creative human output but also intangible aspects of human behaviour such as the growth of a particular habit or manner of behaving within a defined environment.

- It is this culture by which a company will be perceived and judged.
- It is this culture which will determine the reputation of the company.
- It is this culture which will both epitomise and evolve from the way the people in the organisation behave.

A frequent interpretation of culture is 'the way we do things around here'. This phrase reflects what is meant by culture – people behave in a particular manner based around a number of different drivers and stimuli.

Research and consultation undertaken by the FRC and others in recent years, together with a plethora of different publications, have suggested but there is a close alignment between the culture of an organisation and the effective governance of an organisation. The prevailing view goes as far as to suggest that the culture of an organisation can often be set by 'the tone from the top'.

The directors of a company therefore have a significant role in the establishment of an appropriate organisational culture, the maintenance and evolution of that culture, and in ensuring that an optimal culture is reflected from the board behaviour and activities.

NED checklist

- Does the board demonstrate ethical leadership and display the cultural behaviours that are expected from others within the organisation?
- Is the board clear on what sort of culture is needed to underpin the company's purpose and its long-term success?
- How does the board articulate and communicate what is considered to be acceptable business practice?
- Does the board understand the human behaviour that is driving and setting strategic and financial objectives and targets?
- How does our organisational culture relate to our wider stakeholder responsibilities?

Procedure

The 2018 FRC Guidance on Board Effectiveness makes some suggestions with regard to the board's role in establishing and monitoring culture:

- The focus on culture needs to be continuous.
- Periodic reflection on whether the culture continues to be relevant in a changing environment can help the company adapt its culture to ensure it continues to support the company's success.
- The board is expected to assess and monitor culture for alignment with purpose and values. The first step is to establish a benchmark against which future monitoring can take place. One approach to monitoring culture might be to identify and track core characteristics of culture as suggested in the next section and align these with a commitment to company values.

Requirements

- The Guidance suggests the following attributes of a healthy culture:
  - honesty
  - openness
  - respect
  - adaptability
  - reliability
  - recognition

  - acceptance of challenge
  - accountability
  - a sense of shared purpose.
- A board of directors must itself develop a common consistent language around culture, paying attention to factors that can influence culture within the organisation.
- The Guidance further suggests that evidence of culture problems within an organisation might include:
  - silo thinking;
  - a dominant chief executive;
  - leadership arrogance;
  - pressure to meet overambitious targets or numbers;
  - lack of access to information;
  - low levels of meaningful engagement between leadership and employees;
  - lack of openness to challenge;
  - tolerance of regulatory or code of ethics breaches;
  - short term focus; and
  - misaligned incentives.

Further information

- FRC: Guidance on Board Effectiveness (2018).
- FRC: 'Corporate Culture and the Role of Boards'. Available at: www.frc.org.uk/getattachment/3851b9c5-92d3-4695-aeb2-87c9052dc8c1/Corporate-Culture-and-the-Role-of-Boards-Report-of-Observations.pdf.

Cyber risk

Introduction

Cyber risk is identified by the Institute of Risk Management as:

> any risk of financial loss, disruption or damage to the reputation of an organisation from some sort of failure of its information technology systems. Such a risk could materialise in the following ways:
>
> - deliberate and unauthorised breaches of security to gain access to information systems for the purposes of espionage, extortion or embarrassment.
> - unintentional or accidental breaches of security, which nevertheless may still constitute an exposure that needs to be addressed
> - operational IT risks due to poor systems integrity or other factors.

Cyber risk has escalated worldwide as a result of:

- the exponential growth in the use of technology;
- the reliance on technology by many organisations;
- the volumes of data gathered and retained by many organisations;
- the volumes of data held in the 'cloud';
- the number of portable devices capable of accessing data;
- the lack of security on the majority of handheld devices; and
- the ability of criminals to dupe and deceive their victims through the use of both simple and sophisticated technology.

Directors of a business have a duty to ensure that:

- all data gathered and retained by the business is secure, in particular data protected by the General Data Protection Regulation (GDPR); and
- employees have clear policies on the use of the internet, and what is and is not acceptable practice.

NED checklist

- What losses from cyber risk might be catastrophic to your business?
- Does cyber risk feature as a regular part of your risk consideration as directors of the company?
- Do the NEDs hold a similar view of the cyber risk of the company to the executive directors, or does their outside objectivity lead to an increased scepticism?
- Does the organisation have a clear and transparent cyber risk and cybercrime policy? Is this communicated to all employees and do they receive appropriate ongoing training?
- Which aspects of the organisation's technology (if any) could the organisation survive without, and for how long?
- What information that is held by the company must not get into the wrong hands or be made public?
- What might cause personal harm to employees, customers, suppliers, shareholders or other stakeholders?

Procedure

- Understand the risks:
  - Who and what needs to be protected and why?
  - Who are your suppliers and how robust is their cyber security?
  - What are the risks posed by the organisation's supply chain?
- Establish control:
  - set and communicate minimum security requirements to all suppliers;
  - build security considerations into contracting processes and require suppliers to do the same;
  - ensure that the business meets its own security responsibilities as both a supplier and a consumer;
  - raise awareness of cyber security within the supply chain; and
  - provide support for security incidents.
- Check the arrangements:
  - build assurance activities into the approach for managing supply chain risk; and
  - use table-top or other scenario examples to test reaction and capabilities.

- Continuous improvement:
  - encourage the continuous improvement of security within the supply chain; and
  - build trust with suppliers.
- Have a clear, transparent and trained policy with regard to:
  - use of the internet;
  - password creation and change;
  - awareness of and being alert for phishing activities;
  - control of company and personal computers, phones and other internet devices;
  - the security architecture of the organisation; and
  - what an employee should do if they see or receive something suspicious.

Requirements

- It is a requirement of directors that they ensure the safe and continuous running of a business, and the confidential handling of all data. There is a presumed duty of care to employees, and all other stakeholders.

Further information

- The Institute of Risk Management: 'Cyber Risk, Resources for Practitioners' (2014).
- The National Cyber Security Centre, a part of GCHQ, has a range of useful and challenging material available on its website. Available at: www.ncsc.gov.uk.
- The Chartered Governance Institute: guidance note, 'Cyber risk', (2013).

Decision making

Introduction

A board of directors is empowered by the shareholders of the company to use the underlying assets to derive future success. Strategic decisions are therefore an essential, necessary and significantly important part of the work of the board.

The nature of any organisation is that many decisions will be made by many people every single day, it is important for a board of directors to determine which organisational decisions should be made by the directors, and which should be delegated to the operational management and employees of the organisation:

- the former is achieved through the creation of a clear and transparent 'matters reserved for the board' document; and
- the latter is achieved through the creation of a clear and transparent 'scheme of delegations'.

Directors of a company need assurance that decisions are being made from a position of knowledge and understanding, in the best interests of the organisation and avoiding any conflicts of interest.

The FRC Guidance on Board Effectiveness (2018) includes the following comments and advice:

- Well-informed and high-quality decision making does not happen by accident. Many of the factors that lead to poor decision making are predictable and preventable. Boards can minimise the risk of poor decisions by investing time in the design of their decision-making policies and processes, including the contribution of committees and obtaining input from key stakeholders and expert opinions when necessary (paragraph 27).
- Most complex decisions depend on judgment, but the decisions of well-intentioned and experienced leaders can, in certain circumstances, be distorted. Factors known to distort judgment are conflicts of interest, emotional attachments, unconscious bias and inappropriate reliance on previous experience and decisions (paragraph 29).

Once a significant decision has been made and implemented, the board may find it useful to review the effectiveness of the decision-making process and the merits of the decision itself, where it considers it relevant to do so. This could also be considered as part of the board evaluation process.

NED checklist

- Is there clarity on the matters reserved for board decision? Are these contained in a formal publicised document? When was this last reviewed?
- Does a formal 'scheme of delegations' exist within the business? if not, how do the directors of the business know who is making the decisions within the organisation which will commit and risk the assets and reputation of the business?
- As a NED, bringing independence and objectivity to the board table, do you have confidence and assurance that decisions are made by the right people, at the right time, with the right degree of gravitas, throughout the organisation?
- Do you always receive sufficient and appropriate background information and data to enable you, as a director, to make appropriate and informed decisions?
- Are authority levels clearly defined and agreed for the different decisions that are required at different levels throughout the organisation?
- When making significant strategic and impactful decisions do you as a board of directors take sufficient account of your stakeholder responsibilities and accountability under CA2006 s. 172?

Procedure

- The directors should agree which organisational decisions should be made only by the board of directors and these should be reflected in a 'matters reserved for the board' document.
- Decisions that will need be made elsewhere in the business, for the expediency of the day-to-day operational activities of the business, but, where the assets or reputation of the business are placed at risk, should be identified in a formal 'scheme of delegations' document.
- The 'scheme of delegations' should include specific job titles, levels of authority, maximum levels of authorisation and clarity as to how an urgent decision can be escalated to the right person to make a decision.

Notes

- It is always worth considering the type of decision that is about to be made; the consequences of the decision: and the likely impact upon yourself, your organisation, and others. There are three core types of decision:
  - an irreversible decision means that there really is no going back;
  - a reversible decision allows you to go back to the original starting point and rethink; and
  - an experimental, staged or subjective decision is one that 'tests the water' and maybe gives you time before taking an irreversible or reversible decision.
- This level of subliminal detail will be a major influence on your ability to decide; you need to be aware of the potential consequences and impact of our decision making.
- The following questions which can be used to examine your intent when considering the cause and effect of your decision making:
  - Why must you make a decision?
  - Who will your decision affect?
  - Where do you look for help to inform your judgement?
  - What is your personal objective in this situation?
  - When is your deadline?
  - How can you judge the outcome of your decision?

Further information

- The Chartered Governance Institute: guidance note, 'Matters reserved for the board' (for various types of organisations). Available at: www.icsa.org.uk.
- NHS England: 'Annex B: Scheme of Delegation'. Available at: www.england.nhs.uk/wp-content/uploads/2019/09/NHSI_Scheme_of_Delegation_Jul_19_rev_FINAL.pdf.

Derivative claims

Introduction

The duties of a director are owed by the director to the company. Therefore, only the company can bring an action against the director for breach of such duty.

Shareholders have no right to make a direct claim against the director for any loss that they believe they may have suffered as a result of a breach of duty by a director.

However, a company, or the board on behalf of the company, will generally be reluctant to bring a claim against one of its directors.

Over the past 150 years, the law has evolved to enable shareholders to seek the permission of the court to bring a claim against one or more directors in the name of the company.

Such a claim is started and run by the shareholders, but it is brought in the name of the company (and funded by the company) to recover the loss incurred (notionally) by the company as a result of the breach of duty by one or more directors.

This is known as a derivative claim and became a more formalised part of company law in CA2006 ss. 260 to 264.

The ability to bring a derivative claim is not just related to the breach of one of the seven formal duties of a director established under CA2006. It can also relate to any other negligence or legal failure to act appropriately that may have been committed by a director.

A director does not need to have benefited personally from a breach of duty for a derivative claim to be brought.

Present and/or past directors may be pursued under a derivative claim.

Shareholders can also use the derivative claim procedure to pre-emptively prevent an anticipated legal breach of duty.

Any sum for damages levied by a court against a director under a derivative claim will be paid to the company. It is then a company (director) decision as to whether to retain the funds in the company or pay to shareholders by way of dividend.

NED checklist

- Ensure that all directors of the company are aware of their legal duties both under CA2006 and under other legislation such as health and safety law.
- Be aware of how the decisions of directors, and the actions of the company resulting from those decisions, may actually (or in perception) affect or impact upon the varying shareholders of the company.
- Know your shareholders, their resilience to the decisions of the company, and the likelihood of them actively commencing a derivative claim.
- Ensure that directors and officers liability insurance cover is in place to help to fight any such derivative claim. The insurance will not cover the amount of any successful damages awarded against a director or officer, but it will cover the required legal costs, and may cover the quantum of any out-of-court settlement of such a claim.

Procedure

- One or more shareholders who believe a company is failing to take action against a director can issue a claim in the name of the company, requesting the permission of the court to progress and bring the claim in the name of the company against one or more directors.
- The court will expect *prima facie* evidence of damage to the shareholder(s) and will consider:
  - Is it in the best interests of the company for the case to continue or is there an alternative agenda behind the shareholder(s) action?
  - Would a director acting to promote the success of the company themselves bring such a claim against a fellow director?
  - Will the views of, and impact upon, other shareholders be taken into consideration by the court?
- The shareholder(s) initiating any such action risk the costs of the case to that point, being levied against them if the case is not allowed to continue by the court.

Notes

The number of shares held by any shareholder is irrelevant in the bringing of a derivative claim. The reputational damage faced by a company and/or its directors is therefore great and is often the reason that an 'activist' or 'lobbying' shareholder will obtain a single share to enable the initiation of a derivative claim. Even if the shareholder knows in advance that they have no chance of succeeding, the mere bringing of such a claim might cause substantial reputational damage.

Further information

- ICSA Publishing: The Non-Executive Directors' Handbook, chapter 2 (2019)..

Directors and officers insurance

Introduction

One of the common mistakes made by directors of a limited liability company is to believe that it is their liability that is limited. Whereas it is, of course, the liability of the shareholders of the company that is limited.

A director can be held directly accountable for certain decisions and actions of the company such as negligence, corporate manslaughter, failure to follow the duties of a director.

This applies irrespective of the size of company or the nature of the organisation. A director of a large listed company technically holds the same legal liability risks as the director of a small private company, and as the director of a charity.

Under CA2006 a company is not allowed to indemnify its directors. This makes sense as the duty of a director is to the company.

A company is, however, able to obtain directors and officers liability insurance (D&O insurance) as a protection for its directors and officers and to help offset the potential personal costs involved in any legal action that might be brought.

As with any insurance policy, the terms and conditions will vary from policy to policy, so it is important for a NED to know what is covered, when it is covered, and the maximum amount of the liability.

NED checklist

- Does the company have up-to-date and fully paid up D&O insurance?
- If not, why not? Ensure it is on the next board agenda.
- If yes, obtain a copy or summary of the policy to ensure full comprehension of what, when and how much is covered.
- Ensure the policy is reviewed and renewed each year, with any terms, financial limits, reference points and conditions being updated as appropriate (premium is often linked to size and turnover of a company).

Procedure

- The company should:
  - obtain D&O insurance as part of its general maintenance of appropriate and required insurance for the organisation, ensuring that it applies to all its directors and officers;
  - advise directors and officers of the nature and, where appropriate, the details of the policy; and
  - ensure that the policy is renewed on a timely basis, usually annually.

Requirements

- There is no legal requirement for a company to hold D&O insurance.
- It would be usual for directors and officers to insist that D&O insurance is obtained.
- It would be normal practice for this to be referred to in a director's letter of appointment or service contract.

Notes

- What is usually covered by D&O insurance?
  - civil damages awarded against directors;
  - the cost of out-of-court settlements; and
  - costs incurred such as legal fees.
- What is not usually covered by D&O insurance?
  - criminal fines or penalties imposed by a regulator or criminal court;
  - loss of earnings; and
  - liability for fraudulent acts.

Further information

- ICSA Publishing: The Non–Executive Directors' Handbook, Chapter 2 (2019).
- The Chartered Governance Institute: guidance notes, 'Protection against directors' and officers' liabilities – indemnities and insurance'.

Directors' duties

Introduction

Companies Act 2006 s. 170
Scope and nature of general duties

(1) The general duties specified in sections 171 to 177 are owed by a director of a company to the company.

(2) A person who ceases to be a director continues to be subject—

(a) to the duty in section 175 (duty to avoid conflicts of interest) as regards the exploitation of any property, information or opportunity of which he became aware at a time when he was a director, and

(b) to the duty in section 176 (duty not to accept benefits from third parties) as regards things done or omitted by him before he ceased to be a director.

To that extent those duties apply to a former director as to a director, subject to any necessary adaptations.

(3) The general duties are based on certain common law rules and equitable principles as they apply in relation to directors and have effect in place of those rules and principles as regards the duties owed to a company by a director.

(4) The general duties shall be interpreted and applied in the same way as common law rules or equitable principles, and regard shall be had to the corresponding common law rules and equitable principles in interpreting and applying the general duties.

(5) The general duties apply to a shadow director of a company where and to the extent that they are capable of so applying.

Every director of every limited company has a range of general duties which they owe to their company by virtue of their role as a director.

There is no distinction between an executive director and a non-executive director, there is likewise no differentiation between different types of director (e.g. finance director, marketing director, chair of the board, CEO etc).

The core piece of statutory law is the Companies Act 2006. Under this, a duty is owed to the company by anyone who is classed by the Act as a director – this includes formally appointed directors (registered as such at Companies House) and includes people classified as de facto directors or shadow directors.

Until the 2006 Act, duties were based on equity and common law, but a significant part of the law reform was the introduction of seven statutory duties, discussed separately in each of the next main headings.

There are two over riding principles which sit behind all of the formalised duties:

- Fiduciary – a director is being entrusted with the oversight of the assets of the shareholders – the statutory duties add an expectation and structure to this.
- Skill and care – as directors should not act negligently in carrying out their duties. Again, the statutory duties add detail and structure and, in particular s. 174, widen the expectation from the generic (all directors are equal) to the specific (an individual might have an increased duty of care based upon their individual qualifications, background and experience).

NED checklist

- Have you read and understood the statutory duties associated with being a director?
- Have you considered more recent additions and changes to these duties (e.g. the enhanced reporting requirement for s.172)?
- Are you aware of how the company ensures that all directors understand, embody and comply with the expectations of the statutory duties?
- Are you compliant in our reporting expectations with regard to s. 172?
- If you are not registered at Companies House as a formal director, are you nevertheless expected to comply with the statutory duties (i.e. could you be classed as a de facto director or a shadow director)?

Procedure

- Upon appointment as a director of a limited company, each director is sent information from Companies House.

- Ensure that a reconsideration of directors' duties is included at least annually on the board agenda. The only formal statement of compliance is the new enhanced s. 172 reporting for companies classed as large under Companies Act 2006. However, it is good practice for all boards of directors to formally consider their fiduciary accountability and their duty of care.

Further information

- ICSA Publishing: The Non-Executive Directors' Handbook, chapter 2 (2019).
- The Chartered Governance Institute: guidance note. 'Directors' general duties'.
- The Companies Act 2006. Available at: www.legislation.gov.uk/ukpga/2006/ 46/part/10/chapter/2?_ga=2.139268980.655781815.1566553000-1915781761.1565601452.
- Companies House: www.gov.uk/guidance/being-a-company-director.

Directors' duties – duty one

Introduction

> Companies Act 2006 section 171
>
> **Duty to act within powers**
>
> A director of a company must–
>
> (a) act in accordance with the company's constitution, and
> (b) only exercise powers for the purposes for which they are conferred

This duty forms the structural basis for all the other duties owed by directors. The parameters of the duties that are expected from directors are established within the constitution of the company.

Since the implementation of CA 2006, the core document forming the constitution of a company is the articles of association (articles) with the memorandum of association (memorandum) now being a document recognising the initial formation and capital structure of a company.

Although many pre-2006 companies will still have a memorandum, the law would now view all pertinent clauses in such memorandum as being part of the articles.

NED checklist

- Do you have access to a copy of the articles?
- Have you read them?
- Do you understand them, and what is expected from me as a director?
- Have you identified, considered, discussed and challenged any nuances which might seem of particular relevance to this company?
- Have you been appointed in accordance with the articles?

Procedure

- Upon (or ideally before) appointment, make sure you are given access to the articles of association of the company.
- Read carefully and ensure that you understand the operating parameters.
  - If you have not read a set of articles before you may need help from the company secretary, or another director in interpreting some of the clauses.
  - If you are used to the structure of articles then you should be able to look for any unusual or non-standard clauses.

Further information

- ICSA Publishing: The Non-Executive Directors' Handbook, chapter 2 (2019).
- Companies House: model articles of association for limited companies. Available at: www.gov.uk/guidance/model-articles-of-association-for-limited-companies#examples-of-model-articles
- Checklist:Articles of Association, page 8.

Directors' duties – duty two

Introduction

> Companies Act 2006 section 172
>
> **Duty to promote the success of the company**
>
> (1) A director of a company must act in the way he considers, in good faith, would be most likely to promote the success of the company for the benefit of its members as a whole, and in doing so have regard (amongst other matters) to—
>
> (a) the likely consequences of any decision in the long term,
>
> (b) the interests of the company's employees,
>
> (c) the need to foster the company's business relationships with suppliers, customers and others,
>
> (d) the impact of the company's operations on the community and the environment,
>
> (e) the desirability of the company maintaining a reputation for high standards of business conduct, and
>
> (f) the need to act fairly as between members of the company.
>
> (2) Where or to the extent that the purposes of the company consist of or include purposes other than the benefit of its members, subsection (1) has effect as if the reference to promoting the success of the company for the benefit of its members were to achieving those purposes.
>
> (3) The duty imposed by this section has effect subject to any enactment or rule of law requiring directors, in certain circumstances, to consider or act in the interests of creditors of the company.

Each director is individually accountable for their duty to the company. In the context of the growing awareness of the need for governance understanding and principles within private companies, CA2006 s. 172 has been seen as part of the legal building block. While governance is a behavioural expectation rather than a legal requirement, the two concepts are beginning to move ever closer with regard to the accountability to stakeholders of a company.

Directors are faced with the challenging task of owing their duties to the company itself, and yet having to attempt to also take into account the variability and idiosyncrasies not just of the other directors and the shareholders, but also of the wider stakeholder community.

NED checklist

- Have you read and understood the expectation of this duty?
- As a board of directors, how often do you consider the wider stakeholder implications of our decisions?
- Is your stakeholder consideration reflected in the minutes of directors' meetings?
- If applicable to your company, have you considered the wording of the s. 172 reporting requirement (as below), and the impact of your words upon the recipient stakeholder community, and possibly the media?
- Does your culture encourage a wider stakeholder awareness throughout the business, or are you simply paying lip service to an increasing societal expectation?

Requirements

- It is suggested that there are four core drivers that emanate from this directors' duty:
  - Self: an awareness of one's own direct accountability for all decisions being taken.
  - Strategy: that the board must be focused on short and long-term success.
  - Shareholders: that all shareholders must be treated equally.
  - Stakeholders: that the legal duty extends to a wide range of other interested and influential parties.
- The Companies (Miscellaneous Reporting) Regulations 2018 added a more tangible requirement for directors with the addition of the following section into CA2006 s. 414CZA:

  > A strategic report for a financial year of a company must include a statement (a "section 172(1) statement") which describes how the directors have had regard to the matters set out in section 172(1)(a) to (f) when performing their duty under section 172.

- It is referred to as a CA2006 s. 172(1) statement.

- The statement is to be included in the strategic report and made available on the company website.
- This section is applicable to all large companies under CA2006 with effect from financial periods beginning on or after 1 January 2019.
- A large company under CA2006 is defined as one that satisfies two out of three of the following criteria:
  - a turnover of more than £36 million;
  - a balance sheet of more than £18 million; and
  - more than 250 employees.
- For the first time, directors of a significantly larger number of limited companies, not just the listed sector, now have a serious narrative reporting requirement – what is it that we do to comply with the stakeholder expectations, and how can we evidence it?

Further information

- ICSA Publishing: The Non-Executive Directors' Handbook, chapter 2 (2019).
- The Companies Act 2006. Available at: www.legislation.gov.uk/ukpga/2006/46/part/10/chapter/2?_ga=2.139268980.655781815.1566553000-1915781761.1565601452.
- Companies House website: www.gov.uk/guidance/being-a-company-director.

Directors' duties – duty three

Introduction

> Companies Act 2006 section 173
>
> **Duty to exercise independent judgment**
>
> (1) A director of a company must exercise independent judgment.
>
> (2) This duty is not infringed by his acting—
>
> (a) in accordance with an agreement duly entered into by the company that restricts the future exercise of discretion by its directors, or
>
> (b) in a way authorised by the company's constitution

This duty underlines the principle that each director of a company is always acting as an individual.

Even if your appointment as a director is the result of the voting of a particular group of members (e.g. regional, sectoral and so on) the law requires you to act based upon your individual judgement.

This duty does not therefore allow for even the concept of a 'representative director' as has been discussed over recent years.

Notwithstanding the concept of the unitary board (whereby decisions are made in a collective manner) each director must satisfy themselves that they are either in agreement with any particular decision, or (in the case of a split decision requiring a vote) they are prepared (as an individual) to accept the view of the majority.

The concept of independent judgement, in this context, does not necessarily mean that the director is remote from the company or from any decision. It also does not mean that the director is classed as an independent director.

The intent of this duty is to remind each director that they are required to exercise their own independent judgement for each decision being made, and to feel confident to express their own views on any particular matter being addressed by the board.

Each director should be appointed to bring the accumulation of their individual and unique background and knowledge to the wider governance of the company.

Every decision being made by a board of directors is therefore, in effect, a 'joint and several' decision – it is made by the board as a whole, but it is supported, in fact or tacitly, by the independent judgement of each director.

NED checklist

- Have you considered my independence of judgement?
- If you do not agree with a decision that is about to be made by the board of directors, how will you express your views and ensure that your independent opinions are heard by the other directors?
- Do you require my disagreement with a particular decision to be included and identified within the minutes of the meeting? While this will not remove the collective decision-making responsibility, it is possible that it might act as an aspect of personal mitigation if the decision was to ever be challenged in any future legal action.

Procedure

- Make sure that you take the time to consider your own personal views on each issue being addressed by the board of directors.
- Have you expressed your views, either in support or disagreement?
- Are the other directors aware of your views? Should you be trying to persuade them that your approach or opinion is correct?

Further information

- ICSA Publishing: The Non-Executive Directors' Handbook, chapter 2 (2019).

Directors' duties – duty four

Introduction

> Companies Act 2006 section 174
>
> **Duty to exercise reasonable care, skill and diligence**
>
> (1) A director of a company must exercise reasonable care, skill and diligence.
>
> (2) This means the care, skill and diligence that would be exercised by a reasonably diligent person with:
>
> (a) the general knowledge, skill and experience that may reasonably be expected of a person carrying out the functions carried out by the director in relation to the company, and
>
> (b) the general knowledge, skill and experience that the director has.

This addresses the duty of care that is expected from each director in fulfilling their responsibilities.

Prior to the Companies Act 2006, there was an equitable expectation from the law courts that anyone who was, or who appeared to be, a director of a company should behave in a manner that would be deemed as appropriate by 'the man on the Clapham omnibus'. This latter phrase was taken to mean any reasonable person going about their normal business and has been used in a number of legal cases as a benchmark of acceptable behaviour.

The significant change with the implementation of the 2006 Act was the alignment of the **reasonable** expectation with that of a **specific** expectation based upon the individuality of a director.

The test of reasonable care, skill and diligence is therefore twofold:

- What can be expected of any director by the proverbial reasonable person?
- What can be expected of any particular individual director given his or her background, experience and/or profession?

NED checklist

- Have you read and understood the expectation of this duty?
- Have you considered your own background, education, profession etc. and how this might enhance the legal expectation of your role as a director?

Procedure

- Upon appointment, discuss this duty with your fellow directors. Be clear of their expectations from you. What particular and specific skills will they be looking for you to contribute?

Notes

- While this duty does not detract from the perceived joint accountability of a unitary board, it should make each director challenge whether they might be held to have additional knowledge which they should have brought to any discussion or decision.
- This duty might not bring any additional legal liability in any legal case, with each director being held equally accountable as an individual. However, if you have failed to use your experience, knowledge or professional training this is not likely to be viewed well by a judge (or jury).

Further information

- ICSA Publishing: The Non-Executive Directors' Handbook, chapter 2 (2019).

Directors' duties – duty five

Introduction

Companies Act 2006 section 175

Duty to avoid conflicts of interest

(1) A director of a company must avoid a situation in which he has, or can have, a direct or indirect interest that conflicts, or possibly may conflict, with the interests of the company.

(2) This applies in particular to the exploitation of any property, information or opportunity (and it is immaterial whether the company could take advantage of the property, information or opportunity).

(3) This duty does not apply to a conflict of interest arising in relation to a transaction or arrangement with the company.

(4) This duty is not infringed—

(a) if the situation cannot reasonably be regarded as likely to give rise to a conflict of interest; or

(b) if the matter has been authorised by the directors.

(5) Authorisation may be given by the directors—

(a) where the company is a private company and nothing in the company's constitution invalidates such authorisation, by the matter being proposed to and authorised by the directors; or

(b) where the company is a public company and its constitution includes provision enabling the directors to authorise the matter, by the matter being proposed to and authorised by them in accordance with the constitution.

(6) The authorisation is effective only if—

(a) any requirement as to the quorum at the meeting at which the matter is considered is met without counting the director in question or any other interested director, and

> (b) the matter was agreed to without their voting or would have been agreed to if their votes had not been counted.
>
> (7) Any reference in this section to a conflict of interest includes a conflict of interest and duty and a conflict of duties.

Prior to CA2006, it was assumed within common law that a director would not, and should not, be in conflict with their company. The law as applied was a confusion of often conflicting court rulings.

The law reform process believed that a more enlightened approach was required and recognised that conflict will exist and is not always avoidable. This section differentiates between the requirement from the articles between private and public companies and aims to ensure that where conflict is deemed to exist then a fair and equitable process will be followed, in the wider interests of the shareholders and stakeholders of the company.

The starting point is in the first sub-clause with the onus on a director to avoid any situation where they are or may be in conflict with the interests of the company.

NED checklist

- Have you read and understood the expectation of this duty, reviewed whether you have any conflict of interests and reported them to the chair for board approval?
- Does the company and/or the board of directors have a clear and written policy with regard to the handling of conflicts of interest, in addition to and interpreting the practical handling of the statutory legal duty.
- Does the company keep a 'conflicts of interest' register?
- Does the chair of each board or committee meeting start by asking whether any director perceives a conflict of interest on the agenda for that meeting?
- If you are a NED within a public company, have you checked the articles to ensure that an appropriate 'conflicts of interest' clause exists? This is required under the Act, as above.
- If you are a NED within a private company, have you checked the articles to see whether a 'conflicts of interest' clause exists?
- When an actual or apparent conflict of interest arises at the start of a meeting, or during a meeting, is it handled and minuted in the optimal and appropriate manner?
- Does the chair ensure that the conflicted director does not participate in any decision being taken and/or any material aspects of the debate?

Further information

- ICSA Publishing: The Non-Executive Directors' Handbook, chapter 2 (2019).
- The Companies Act 2006. Available at: www.legislation.gov.uk/ukpga/2006/46/part/10/chapter/2?_ga=2.139268980.655781815.1566553000-1915781761.1565601452.
- Companies House website: www.gov.uk/guidance/being-a-company-director.

Directors' duties – duty six

Introduction

Companies Act 2006 section 176

Duty not to accept benefits from third parties

(1) A director of a company must not accept a benefit from a third party conferred by reason of—

(a) his being a director, or

(b) his doing (or not doing) anything as director.

(2) A 'third party' means a person other than the company, an associated body corporate or a person acting on behalf of the company or an associated body corporate.

(3) Benefits received by a director from a person by whom his services (as a director or otherwise) are provided to the company are not regarded as conferred by a third party.

(4) This duty is not infringed if the acceptance of the benefit cannot reasonably be regarded as likely to give rise to a conflict of interest.

(5) Any reference in this section to a conflict of interest includes a conflict of interest and duty and a conflict of duties.

The purpose of this duty was, and is, to challenge a director to consider whether any benefit being received from a stakeholder of the company, or any other third party, is as a result of being a director of the company.

There does not need to be any malicious intent on the part of the donor of the benefit, nor any assumed connivance on the part of the director. The intention of the duty is to protect the director and the company from any actual or perceived conflict of interest arising as a result of such a gift.

How far does this need to go in reality? Taking a bribe is clearly wrong, but what about accepting an expensive lunch, or accepting an invitation to a major sporting event? A line needs to be drawn by each company as to what is and is not acceptable, given the nature of the business and the relationships that exist. A court of law is likely to take the view of a reasonable and unconnected third party – how would that person view the giving and receiving of such a gift? In theory, no harm needs to be proved, simply that a conflict of interest may have resulted as a result of the acceptance by the director.

NED checklist

- Have you read and understood the expectation of this duty?
- Does the company have a clear company policy with regard to the acceptance of benefits, invitations, or other gifts from a stakeholder of the company and/or any other third party?
- If the receiving of gifts etc. is allowed by the company within certain criteria or circumstances, is a register kept of all such gifts to ensure openness and transparency from all directors in this regard?
- Is there a consistency amongst directors in the way in which they interpret this duty – remembering that the law draws no distinction between an executive director and a NED – a director is a director?

Notes

- The Bribery Act 2010 underlines many of the principles intended by this duty but extends it to all and any employee of the organisation.

Further information

- ICSA Publishing: The Non-Executive Directors' Handbook, chapter 2 (2019).
- Checklist: Bribery Act 2010, page 39.
- The Companies Act 2006: Available at: www.legislation.gov.uk/ukpga/2006/ 46/part/10/chapter/2?_ga=2.139268980.655781815.1566553000-1915781761.1565601452.
- Companies House website: www.gov.uk/guidance/being-a-company-director.

Directors' duties – duty seven

Introduction

Companies Act 2006 section 177

Duty to declare interest in proposed transaction or arrangement

(1) If a director of a company is in any way, directly or indirectly, interested in a proposed transaction or arrangement with the company, he must declare the nature and extent of that interest to the other directors.

(2) The declaration may (but need not) be made—

(a) at a meeting of the directors, or

(b) by notice to the directors in accordance with—

(i) section 184 (notice in writing), or

(ii) section 185 (general notice).

(3) If a declaration of interest under this section proves to be, or becomes, inaccurate or incomplete, a further declaration must be made.

(4) Any declaration required by this section must be made before the company enters into the transaction or arrangement.

(5) This section does not require a declaration of an interest of which the director is not aware or where the director is not aware of the transaction or arrangement in question.

For this purpose, a director is treated as being aware of matters of which he ought reasonably to be aware.

(6) A director need not declare an interest—

(a) if it cannot reasonably be regarded as likely to give rise to a conflict of interest;

(b) if, or to the extent that, the other directors are already aware of it (and for this purpose the other directors are treated as aware of anything of which they ought reasonably to be aware); or

> (c) if, or to the extent that, it concerns terms of his service contract that have been or are to be considered (i) by a meeting of the directors, or (ii) by a committee of the directors appointed for the purpose under the company's constitution.

This lengthy final duty is, in essence, quite straightforward. Following the principle established in s. 175 (Duty five) that a director should not have a conflict of interest with the company or its business, s. 175(3) states 'this duty does not apply to a conflict of interest arising in relation to a transaction or arrangement with the company'. Thus, the onus within s. 177 (Duty 7) is placed upon the director to ensure that they notify that company and their fellow directors of any conflict, or perceived conflict, that they know exists in any current or future transaction of the company.

Having so notified the company, the constitution should contain an appropriate clause determining whether that director is still entitled to participate in debate and/or vote on any material decision where an actual or apparent conflict may exist or may be perceived to exist.

NED checklist

- Have you read and understood the expectation of this duty?
- Do the articles of the company give clear direction with regard to participation in meetings and/or voting where an actual or perceived conflict exists?
- Does the chair of a board or committee meeting check with the meeting attendees whether they are aware of the existence of any actual or perceived conflict?
- When any such conflict is advised before, during (or even after) a meeting, is there a record or register kept of such conflicts, thus providing transparency and an audit trail, if the decision of discussion was ever to be challenged?

Further information

- ICSA Publishing: The Non-Executive Directors' Handbook, chapter 2 (2019).
- The Companies Act 2006: Available at: www.legislation.gov.uk/ukpga/2006/ 46/part/10/chapter/2?_ga=2.139268980.655781815.1566553000-1915781761.1565601452.
- Companies House website: www.gov.uk/guidance/being-a-company-director.

Directors' report

Introduction

Companies Act 2006 (the Act) s. 415 requires the directors of limited companies (other than companies classified as a 'micro-entity) to provide a directors' report for each financial year of the company.

The directors' report for a company classified as a 'small company' must still be provided but has many exemptions as identified below.

The report will form part of the annual report and accounts that are submitted to Companies House. Failure to provide such a report as and when required is an offence under the Act, committed by every person who was a director immediately before the end of the period for filing of accounts and reports for the financial year in question.

NED checklist

- Has the latest annual report and account for the current year end been discussed and considered in the light of changes in the company during the year?
- Does the directors' report contain all statutory requirements?
- Are the NEDS made aware of the procedure for the writing and completion of the next directors' report?
- Is reporting treated as part of the annual cycle or does the process become rushed as dead-lines approach?
- Remember that a NED has an equal liability with all other directors of the company to ensure full compliance with the Act with regards to accounting reporting.

Requirements

The directors' report from a 'small company' must include:

- the names of directors during the financial year;

- if the company has been audited, then there should be a statement from the directors concerning the information provided to the auditors;
- approval by and signature on behalf of the board of directors;
- a statement confirming the use of the small companies' exemptions;
- information on any political donations and expenditure in excess of £2,000; and
- a statement on the policy regarding employment of disabled persons if the average weekly number of UK-based employees exceeds 250.

The directors' report from all other limited companies must include:

- the names of directors during the financial year;
- the recommended final dividend payment for the financial year;
- a statement concerning the information provided to the auditors by the directors;
- approval by and signature on behalf of the board of directors;
- identification of any directors' report requirements that have instead been included in the strategic report;
- information on any political donations and expenditure in excess of £2,000;
- the objectives and policies of financial risk management undertaken by the company;
- details of any exposure to price risk, credit risk, liquidity risk and/or cashflow risk;
- details of any post-balance sheet events (aspects of the business which have occurred in the following financial year and might materially affect the views or opinions of the shareholders or stakeholders on the financial standing and/or prospects of the company;
- likely future development in the business of the company;
- research and development being undertaken by the company;
- a statement confirming whether any of the company's shares have been repurchased by the company;
- a statement on the policy regarding employment of disabled persons if the average weekly number of UK-based employees exceeds 250; and
- a description of employee involvement policies if the average weekly number of UK-based employees exceeds 250.

Additionally, where the company is a quoted company

- detailed information on the capital structure of the company; and
- details of greenhouse gas emissions including a ratio relationship between emissions and company activity must be provided.

Further information

- The Companies Act 2006. Available at: www.legislation.gov.uk/ukpga/2006/46/part/10/chapter/2?_ga=2.139268980.655781815.1566553000-1915781761.1565601452.

Dividends

Introduction

Unless shares of any particular class carry a fixed dividend, the declaration and payment of a dividend are at the directors' discretion – as set out in the company's constitution.

Dividends can be paid only if the company has sufficient distributable profits either from the current financial year or retained from previous financial years.

In the case of an interim dividend, the directors may declare a dividend as they see fit in line with the financial performance of the company.

In the case of the final dividend for a financial year, such dividend is proposed in the context of any interim dividend(s) that have been declared during the financial year in question. The final dividend needs the approval of the members of the company by ordinary resolution, either at an AGM, or through written circulation of the proposal in a private company that has elected not to have an AGM.

The declaration of any dividend should be made by reference to the relevant accounts. These would normally be the most recent annual accounts except where those accounts show that there is insufficient profit available or the dividend is proposed to be paid in the first accounting period. In such cases, interim or initial accounts, as appropriate, will be required. If the annual accounts have a qualified auditors' report, the auditor must issue a statement about whether the qualification is material for determining if a distribution can be made in terms of s. 836 of CA2006.

For a private company, the interim or initial accounts must enable a reasonable judgement to be made as to the availability of distributable reserves.

For a public company, those accounts must be properly prepared in accordance with ss. 395, 396 and 397 of CA2006. Where interim accounts are prepared, these must be signed, and a copy filed with the registrar of companies.

NED checklist

- Although conceptually the payment of a dividend is the result of declaring profitability, directors should determine, as part of their financial strategy and planning, the intended dividend policy and payments against the financial projections for a particular financial year. Does this happen as part of the financial budgeting and projection process?
- Are the NEDs actively involved in the formulation of the dividend strategy? Do you have the opportunity to challenge and question the nature and quantum of such a policy?
- In a listed company (or a private company with a public interest dimension), do you understand, debate and challenge the likely reputational, media and shareholder impact of declaring dividends at a particular level?
- Are you satisfied that the company is declaring or proposing dividends that are fully financed by distributable profits either from the current financial year or retained from previous financial years?
- Has the liquidity implication of the timing and quantum of a dividend declaration or proposal been fully considered? Might it impact the going concern nature of the company?

Procedure

- Interim dividend.
  - Convene a directors' meeting to consider the payment of an interim dividend.
  - Consider the impact on the company liquidity and adequacy of e-distributable profit by reference to relevant accounts.
  - Declare the dividend to the members indicating both the declaration date and the payment date.
- Final dividend.
  - Issue the accounts and notice of general meeting to the members. If accounts have a qualified audit report, ensure the auditors' statement on their qualification is circulated with the accounts.
  - Hold the general meeting. Or alternatively, circulate the proposal to the members of a private company that has elected not to hold an AGM.
  - If approval is given to the final dividend, payment can be arranged in the same way as for an interim dividend.
  - Although members can reduce the amount of dividend payable, they cannot approve a payment at a higher rate than that recommended by the directors.

Dormant companies

Introduction

Where a company has not traded during any particular financial period it can be classed as a dormant company. The directors can dispense with the obligation to prepare audited accounts and need only file an abbreviated balance sheet and notes with Companies House.

NED checklist

- Check if there are any dormant companies within the group. There must have been no transactions made, or required to have been made, in the company's accounts during the financial period in question.
- If part of a group, the dormant accounts must continue to be included in the group consolidated accounts.
- The balance sheet must be signed in the normal manner to reflect the dormant status, the responsibilities of the directors, the true and fair nature of the dormant accounts and that the members have not required an audit.

Procedure

- Non-trading, non-audited accounts must be prepared.
- The accounts must still be approved by the directors of the company.
- A signed copy of the dormant accounts must be filed within the normal timescales (six months for a public company and nine months for a private company).
- An annual confirmation statement must continue to be filed with Companies House.

Notes

- For a company to remain dormant, any costs must be paid by someone other than the company itself and any cash held in a bank must be in a non-interest-bearing account.
- Receipt of payment by the company for the shares taken by the subscribers or any payment made in respect of any change of name, re-registration fees, annual returns or late filing penalties may be disregarded for the purposes of assessing whether a company is dormant.
- Although the copy of the accounts that is filed with the registrar may be abbreviated and need not contain a directors' report, the copy circulated to shareholders must be full accounts including a directors' report.

Due diligence – becoming a NED

Introduction

The role of a NED brings with it high levels of expectation along with the statutory and other duties of a director. The role should never be undertaken and accepted without firstly undertaking an appropriate level of due diligence.

Due diligence refers to the process of investigating, auditing, or researching the background to any required decision. In this instance that of taking on the responsibilities and liabilities of being a NED.

The Higgs Review in 2003 first suggested that a prospective director should undertake their own thorough examination of a company to satisfy themselves that it is an organisation in which they could have confidence and are happy to serve as a NED.

NED checklist

- Who owns and controls the company? Who are the shareholders?
- What is the level of bank borrowing? What other long and short-term financial commitments exist?
- Who is the chair, who are the other NEDs and who are the other directors? What is the level of experience, professionalism and expertise around the table? What levels of independence exist?
- What will I bring to the board of directors? What are they expecting from me?
- Do I foresee any conflicts of interest with the company, its directors, its subsidiaries, its suppliers and customers?
- What is the risk profile of the company?
- What is the reputation and culture of the company? How is it viewed by its stakeholders?

Procedure

- Review the latest Companies House information on the company to assess the legal structure, ownership structure and director structure.
- Obtain and review the articles of association and any other structural documents.
- Obtain and review the annual report and accounts for at least the last two years.
- Having signed an appropriate non-disclosure agreement, obtain and review board agenda, minutes and board papers for the past year.
- Arrange to meet the chair, the company secretary and at least two of the other directors on a one-to-one basis – these face-to-face discussions can be the most productive research into whether this is the right company for you to become a NED.
- In your review and consideration of the financial stability of the company (ensure you review HMRC status and check that all payments are up-to-date) and levels and terms of any bank borrowing.
- Research the company online, and, if relevant and appropriate, talk to major customers, suppliers or other stakeholders.

Further information

- The Chartered Governance Institute guidance note: 'Joining the right board: due diligence for prospective directors'. This document contains a detailed checklist of due diligence questions for prospective NEDs to consider

Due diligence – board decisions

Introduction

Directors of a company are empowered and required to make decisions which will deplete and/or risk the assets of the company (ultimately the assets of the shareholders) with a view to running the operation of the business and promoting the success of the company.

Due diligence refers to the process of investigating, auditing, or researching the background to any required decision that will deplete and/or risk a material value of the assets of the company. This includes receiving assurance of the veracity, integrity and truth of the data and information being used to enable a decision to be made.

The level of materiality that should require a due diligence process will be determined from time to time by the directors and/or shareholders of a company. This should align with the key performance indicators (KPIs) and other metrics used by the board of directors.

Directors need to ensure that appropriate due diligence is carried out on all aspects of their supply chain. Section 172 of CA2006 requires directors of a company to 'foster the company's business relationships with suppliers, customers and others' when making decisions about the success of the company.

Due diligence is also advised with regard to a broad range of other areas such as:

- mitigation of risk under the Bribery Act 2010 and under the Modern Slavery Act 2015;
- potential acquisitions; and
- investment of liquid assets.

Due diligence can, therefore, be seen as a fundamental requirement in the building of protection for the directors of a company.

NED checklist

- Can the directors show that they have undertaken every possible line of due diligence enquiry with regard to all key and material decisions?
- Is there clarity on the quantitative levels that are to be used to judge materiality of decisions?
- Do all material decisions come to the board of directors? How do you know (ignorance is no defence in law)?
- Does the company have a robust policy for undertaking due diligence across its supply chain?
- How often are customers and suppliers reviewed from financial and reputational perspectives?
- Does the company have due diligence policies and are they clear? Do any such policies protect the company's interests adequately in line with any relevant legislation or expectations of directors and company stakeholders?

E-commerce

Introduction

A dictionary definition of e-commerce is the 'business of buying and selling goods and services on the internet'. The objective of e-commerce is to increase the competitiveness and efficiency of a business by using electronic information exchange to improve processes.

This is far more than automating existing processes. Intelligent e-commerce will often require radical rethinking and redesign of processes to maximise the potential of electronic methods bringing greater efficiency and adding more value.

E-commerce can evolve the current markets where goods and services are traded by a company. The marketplace can be widened to include a more global customer reach, but also it can be narrowed to ensure very specific focusing of a particular product or service to a particular range of customers.

E-commerce will change the nature of relationships with suppliers and customers.

E-commerce includes many categories of partner: business to customer (B2C) such as Amazon, or IKEA, business to business (B2B) such as ADP, customer to business (C2B) such as crowd funding, consumer to consumer (C2C) (e.g. Ebay), government to consumer (G2C), government to business (G2B) and consumer to government (C2G). The latter categories include transactions where taxes, services or fines are disclosed, provided and paid online.

It is likely that your business will already be involved in a wide range of e-commerce activities. An example of this is the move to 'Making Tax Digital' by HMRC where all companies are required to submit performance details electronically to HMRC, hence the tax due becomes a derived figure. Likewise, the majority of returns to Companies House are now required to be submitted online.

The major issues for directors to consider from a governance perspective are related control and privacy. E-commerce brings enhanced risk and the potential for a wide range of people other than the intended stakeholders to gain information on the operations and activities of a business. It is for this reason that alongside the exponential growth of e-commerce we have seen a large growth in the need for cyber-crime awareness.

NED checklist

- Do you have clarity on all areas where your business is involved in e-commerce?
- Does your risk register, or equivalent, feature e-commerce and the associated risk of cyber crime?
- How reliant is your business on e-commerce? If all systems failed, would you still be able to trade?
- Are you maximising the potential for simplification and added-value through the use of e-ecommerce in your business and within your sector?
- At what level does your business use technology?
- Does your longer-term strategy envisage an increased use of technology?

Procedure

- The development of an effective e-commerce capability can involve a gradual (if rapid) staged process build.
  - Web-presence – online representation of the company and its products and services.
  - E-commerce – the use of online technology to enable and fulfil trading contracts.
  - Integrated e commerce – the gathering and building of data to enable predictive commercial activities
  - E-business – the business strategy is driven by and/or dependent upon the use of technology to enable trade.

Electronic communications

Introduction

The control and practice of electronic communications between the company and its directors and between directors should be set out in the articles of association (articles) and/or any directors or board procedures documents. As there is no statutory requirement for these communications, each company can evolve a practice that is appropriate for its size, complexity and geographical diversity of directors.

Subject to any provisions in the articles, and obtaining shareholder consent under Schedule 5 to CA2006, a company may send written resolutions, notices, annual accounts and related documents to their members in hard copy, in electronic form or by making the documents available for download from a website.

Quoted companies are required to make their annual report and accounts available on a website as soon as reasonably practical.

Any member receiving documents or information by electronic communication or by publication on a website can request that they receive copies of documents in hard copy and the company must supply those copies within 21 days.

NED checklist

- Does the company have a clear and appropriate policy for the use of electronic communication with and between directors?
- Is the control of electronic communication part of the cyber risk policy of the company, and is it appropriate for the size, complexity and required confidentiality of such communications?
- Has the company obtained specific or general consent from its directors to use electronic communication?
- Has the company obtained specific or general consent from its shareholders to use electronic communication for shareholder matters, including the making available on a website relevant documents and information? In a listed company such consent must be received in a general meeting.

Further information

The Chartered Governance Institute: guidance note, 'Electronic communications with shareholders' (2013).

The Chartered Governance Institute: guidance note, 'Good practice for virtual board and committee meetings' (2020).

Enterprise risk management

Introduction

Enterprise risk management (ERM) is defined by the Committee of Sponsoring Organizations of the Treadway Commission (COSO) as:

> A process, effected by an entity's board of directors, management and other personnel, applied in strategy setting and across the enterprise, designed to identify potential events that may affect the entity, and manage risk to be within its risk appetite, to provide reasonable assurance regarding the achievement of entity objectives.

Three key characteristics distinguish an ERM process from a standard risk management process.

- A holistic focus – ERM will include all types of risk across every part of an organisation, recognising that different risks, functions, business lines and processes are all interconnected.
- An emphasis on value addition through risk management – when applied correctly, ERM will create and protect value within an organisation through effective strategic-level risk management decision making, and operations that function smoothly without costly interruption
- A blending of formal and informal risk management tools and activities – ERM requires a holistic approach recognising that tangible systems need to align with informal influences within the organisation.
  - Tangible systems will include the processes, procedures, policies, committees and forums that exist within the organisation, together with the structure and hierarchy in the risk-decision control process.
  - Informal influences on risk will include aspects of the business such as organisational culture and social networks, both internal and external.

NED checklist

- Does the organisation have a formal approach to risk management?
- Has the board of directors considered adopting an ERM approach, either in total or in concept?
- Does the risk management process of the organisation deliver value-addition and enable a holistic focus on all aspects of risk within the organisation?
- Is it clear who within the organisation is accountable to the board of directors for risk oversight and control?
- As a NED, do you receive sufficient and regular information on all matters pertaining to the risks within the organisation at an appropriate level of granularity?
- Are you encouraged to bring an objective and challenging perspective to the consideration of risk within the organisation?

Notes

The perceived benefits of ERM are:

- improved reporting to support strategic decision making;
- avoidance of silos;
- improved operational efficiency and cost effectiveness;
- improved profitability and equity value;
- improved ability to achieve other business objectives;
- consistent decision making;
- effective resource allocation for risk management; and
- spreading risk ownership, allowing risks to be managed by the local experts.

Further information

- Committee of Sponsoring Organizations of the Treadway Commission. Available at: www.coso.org

ESG responsibilities

Introduction

In our corporate world, there continues to be a global drive towards a more enhanced accountability and reporting aligned with the already recognised corporate social responsibility of organisations.

This drive has been aligned with wider governance expectations under the acronym ESG:

- Environmental – the company's impact on the earth;
- Social – how the company manages relationships with employees, clients, suppliers and communities; and
- Governance – company oversight, internal controls, treatment of stakeholders, alignment of business success and management reward.

The three central factors of ESG help measure the social impact and sustainability of an investment in a company, and determine the future financial performance of a company. It is for this reason that ESG has become popular with investors to help them evaluate whether they want to invest in a particular company.

As often happens, this acronym is now being used as a prefix to many other corporate concepts such as:

- ESG criteria
- ESG approach
- ESG reporting
- ESG culture
- ESG investing.

As this approach becomes encompassing within many aspects of the life of an organisation, it is through the narrative reporting that shareholders and stakeholders will be able to form their judgements as to the genuine approach being taken by an organisation.

Discussion of sustainability and finance has increasingly infiltrated aspects of corporate life across the past 25 years. This has been apparent in accounting literature and the expanding transparent reporting expectation in an organisation's annual report and accounts. This has been epitomised by the move to a wider stakeholder economy and the need and/or desire for organisations, of all shape and size, to recognise and be accountable for their duty of care to society.

NED checklist

- Has the board discussed its ESG approach alongside sustainability and do you report on these?
- Is ESG recognised as a wider accountability than CSR?
- As a NED, and therefore not weighed down by the daily politics of the organisation, how can you more effectively challenge the ESG norm?
- What are the tangible and intangible measures that evidence your organisation's approach?
- What would you say to an activist shareholder when challenged about the ESG approach of the organisation?
- Do any ESG measures form part of your regular board metrics?
- Do your published year-end KPIs include any ESG dimension?

Procedure

- Whatever the formal structure of an organisation, directors are accountable to a wide range of stakeholders. Directors need to be able to understand the impact of organisational decisions on the world and its people. This should be made an aspect of all core board decisions.
- The board should consider:
  - the company's ESG (i.e. its environmental impact, how it manages relationships, treats stakeholders, its oversight, management and internal controls);
  - the ethical norms and behaviour that can or cannot be expected from within the organisation;
  - the behaviours that can be expected by stakeholders from the organisation, within the context of the sector;
  - the manner in which employees of the organisation are treated;
  - the ethics and ethos that pervade the organisation – ethics being the behavioural traits that are visible and ethos being the ethical stance being taken by those who structure and oversee the culture within an organisation; and
  - how all of the above impact and support sustainability internally and externally.

Requirements

- Directors of a company classed as large under CA2006 are required to include a s. 172 report as part of the strategic report. This requires commentary as to how the directors have addressed their stakeholder responsibilities, including commentary on the impact of the company's operations on the community and the environment.
- Large companies are currently expected to report on their approaches to gender diversity, disability and modern slavery.
- The 2018 UK Corporate Governance Code enhances the expectations from listed companies on their tangible and evidenced wide engagement with the workforce of the company.
- Directors of a listed company have enhanced reporting requirements including carbon and greenhouse gas emissions
- The UK Government Green Finance Strategy established a Task Force on Climate-related Financial Disclosures (TCFD). Under this initiative, the UK Government expects all listed companies and large asset owners to be disclosing in line with the TCFD recommendations by 2022. These are:
  - the organisation's governance around climate-related risks and opportunities;
  - the actual and potential impacts of climate-related risks and opportunities on the organisation's business, strategy, and financial planning;
  - the process used by the organisation to identify, assess, and manage climate related risks; and
  - the metrics and targets used to assess and manage relevant climate related risks and opportunities.

Notes

- A group of major organisations and investors (under the title EPIC – Embankment Project for Inclusive Capital), together controlling over $30tn of assets, is calling on companies to be more open and transparent about their non-financial assets such as staffing, governance, innovation and their impact on society and the environment.
- One 'buzz phrase' that attempts to capture these concepts within a financial framework was the development in 1994 of a 'triple bottom line' (TBL) approach. It is suggested that TBL captures the essence of sustainability by allowing an organisation to measure the impact of its activities on the world; with a positive TBL indicating an increase in profitability, shareholder value and the social, human, and environmental capital associated with that organisation. This links very closely with ESG by referring to similar issues. One problem

with the TBL approach is that it develops a range of potential silos, where it is difficult to add up the ultimate benefits. Further, it is challenging to measure the differing aspects of sustainability from a purely monetary or numeric dimension.

Further information

- UK Government: 'Green Finance Report'. Available at: assets.publishing.service.gov.uk/government/uploads/system/uploads/attachment_data/file/820284/190716_BEIS_Green_Finance_Strategy_Accessible_Final.pdf
- Embankment Project for Inclusive Capital (EPIC). Available at: www.epic-value.com.

Financial duties and accountabilities

Introduction

Directors are responsible for the operation of the company on behalf of the shareholders. Given the expectation of promoting the long-term success of the company for the members, directors must take upon themselves financial oversight, financial accountability and financial control of the company.

The level of financial involvement and the depth of financial expectation will depend on the size of the company (CA2006, s. 380) but there is a statutory legal requirement for all directors to ensure that the company keeps 'adequate accounting records' (CA2006, s. 386). A criminal offence is committed by each director and officer of a company if the accounting records are not deemed to be adequate within any financial period (CA2006, s. 387).

NED checklist

- You need to be satisfied that the company is maintaining adequate accounting records by maintaining a suitable and appropriate accounting system. This should record, show and explain the financial transactions of the company and be able to reflect, at any time, with 'reasonable accuracy', the financial position of the company at that time.
- Directors are required to ensure that the accounts of the company comply with CA2006 and International Accounting Standards (as appropriate for the size of company). Section 386 of CA2006 specifies that such records must contain:
    - day-to-day entries of all sums of money received and expended by the company and the matters in respect of which the receipt and expenditure takes place (normally satisfied through the provision of income and expenditure, or profit and loss accounts); and
    - a record of the assets and liabilities of the company (normally satisfied through the provision of a balance sheet).

- In addition to this requirement, you should regularly review the solvency of the company through requesting, challenging and understanding the cashflows of the company, both current and projected.

Procedure

- Directors must keep a constant awareness of the liquidity of the company. It is a criminal offence for directors to continue to trade if they are aware that the company is insolvent and is unable to continue to make the day-to-day payments required to operate the business. In such circumstances, directors (NEDS and EDs) can be held personally liable for the debts of the company.
- The annual accounts of each company, irrespective of size, must be approved by the directors of the company and presented to the members; this might be a formal or an informal procedure depending on the size of company and the expectation of its members. Section 393 of CA2006 states that:

> Directors of a company must not approve the accounts unless they are satisfied that they give a true and fair view of the assets, liabilities, financial position and profit or loss of the company or group.

Notes

- This checklist should be read in conjunction with the other financially focused checklists included in this text.

Financial literacy – balance sheet

Introduction

The balance sheet (or statement of financial position) of a company reflects the assets and liabilities of that company at any specific moment in time. It is often referred to as a 'financial snapshot' of the company and it is designed to be exactly that.

Remember that the majority of the numbers included on a balance sheet will have been subject to one or more human judgements. A core NED role is to be aware of and be prepared and ready to constructively challenge those judgements.

A company asset is a resource **owned** or controlled by the company that has an immediate cash value or is expected to provide a future cash **inflow** to the company.

A company liability is anything that is **owed** by a company to someone else and is expected to require a future cash **outflow** from the company.

The annual report and accounts of a company is expected to include a balance sheet as at the financial year end of the company. Even in a micro company, it is the balance sheet which is filed at Companies House.

It is good practice, a part of the wider financial duties of directors, for a balance sheet to be produced as part of each period end (monthly or quarterly) financial information pack.

NED checklist

- Are key aspects of the balance sheet, such as working capital, provided as part of the management information on a regular basis?
- Does the financial director regularly discuss the core solvency aspects of the balance sheet – inventory, debtors, creditors, cash, borrowings?
- Do the NEDs regularly discuss the balance sheet provided to monitor the financial position of the company?

Structure

In the UK, we generally use a 'straight form' balance sheet with the following outline structure.

A Non-current assets

Tangible (eg Buildings, Plant and equipment)
Intangible (eg Goodwill, IP, Brand names)

B Current assets *(expected to become cash within 12 months from Balance Sheet date)*

Inventory (raw materials, work-in-progress, finished goods)
Trade and other debtors (people who owe money to the company)
Bank and cash

C Current liabilities *(expected to become cash within 12 months from Balance Sheet date)*

Trade and other creditors (people we owe money to)
HMRC (PAYE, VAT, Corporation tax)
Bank borrowings

D Non-current liabilities

Longer term bank and other borrowings

NET WORTH OF THE COMPANY (A + B - C - D)

The net worth balances with the shareholder funds

E Share Capital
Retained profits
Other reserves

SHAREHOLDER FUNDS E = (A + B - C - D)

The structure is altered to directly compare assets and liabilities in Europe, the USA and most of the rest of the world.

A Non-current assets Tangible (eg Buildings, Plant and equipment) Intangible (eg Goodwill, IP, Brand names)	**E Share Capital** Retained profits Other reserves **D Non-current liabilities** Longer term bank and other borrowings
B Current assets *(expected to become cash within 12 months from Balance Sheet date)* Inventory (raw materials, work-in-progress, finished goods) Trade and other debtors (people who owe money to the company) Bank and cash	**C Current liabilities *(expected to become cash within 12 months from Balance Sheet date)*** Trade and other creditors (people we owe money to) HMRC (PAYE, VAT, Corporation tax) Bank borrowings
TOTAL ASSETS OF THE COMPANY (A + B)	**= TOTAL LIABILITIES OF THE COMPANY (E + D + C)**

Financial literacy – cash flow statement

Introduction

The cash flow statement of a company reflects the cash movements within a timed trading period with a start and end date, for example:

- Periodic – The week ending 30 September 2019 or the month of September 2019.
- Cumulative – The period from 1 January to 30 September 2019.
- Annual – 1 October 2018 to 30 September 2019.

The purpose is to show the cash received by the company during that period set against the cash that has been paid by the company during that period – the difference being an increase or reduction in cash.

When aligned to the balance sheet of the company, the figures can be reconciled.

- Opening balance sheet cash position
- Adjusted by the increase or reduction in cash during the period
- Equals
- Closing balance sheet cash position

It is usual to reflect the cash movements during the period within these main headings:

- Cash flows generated from or used in **operating** activities
  - The cash movements resulting from trading.
- Cash flows generated from or used in **investing** activities
  - The cash movements resulting from purchase or sale of assets.
- Cash flows generated from or used in **financing** activities
  - The cash movements resulting from borrowing and/or repaying bank or other loans, raising share capital and paying dividends.

The total of the three activities will produce the net increase or decrease in cash for the period. This figure can be used to reconcile the opening cash position and closing cash position.

NED checklist

- Is a cash flow statement and forecast provided as part of the management information on a regular basis?
- Does the financial director regularly discuss the core aspects of the cash flow statement and comment on any unusual movements or trends?
- When the financial year-end cash flow statement is provided, is there a clear bridge of items that differ between the financial accounts and the management accounts?
- Do the NEDs discuss liquidity and cash flow on a regular basis?
- Do the NEDs have clarity on the solvency and liquidity position of the company both short- and long-term? Are the NEDs provided with sufficient information about the activities and movements of cash flows and the cash position of the company. If the company carries on trading whilst insolvent, the directors may be held liable for wrongful trading.

Financial literacy – income statement

Introduction

The income statement (or statement of profit or loss and other comprehensive income) of a company reflects the revenues and expenses of a timed trading period with a start and end date, for example:

- Periodic – The week ending 30 September 2019 or the month of September 2019
- Cumulative – The period from 1 January to 30 September 2019
- Annual – 1 October 2018 to 30 September 2019.

The purpose is to show the income (or revenue) generated for that period against the costs that have been incurred to enable that income to be generated (expenses). Note this is carefully worded – the income statement reflects trading movements, not cash movements.

The difference is the income and the costs being the profit or loss generated during the period.

Income generated is reflected from the invoices raised during a period (the tax-point or the point where title is transferred) adjusted for the value of invoices raised for work not yet completed and/or work that has been completed and could have been invoiced. This will provide an audit trail to verify the income figure.

Costs that need to be set against that income may comprise several categories. These will provide an audit trail to prove the cost figure.

- Direct costs: costs that have been incurred which directly relate to the cost of production of the sale of the products and/or services recognised in the 'income' figure for the period (e.g. raw materials consumed, labour costs incurred, packaging etc). These direct costs usually have a direct proportionate relationship with each unit of product or service (e.g. volume, number of hours etc).
- Indirect costs: all other costs incurred by the business where a proportion of that cost has helped to provide the infrastructure which has allowed the production of the product or service (e.g. management and director salaries, accounts and HR, equipment depreciation etc).

- Adjustments that need to be made to reflect:
  - costs incurred that have not yet been invoiced by suppliers (these are often referred to as accruals); and
  - costs incurred that relate to a longer period of time, or period of production than the period covered by the specific income statement (these are often referred to as prepayments).

Terms are often used in slightly different ways by businesses. At the management accounting level each company can produce its own variant of structure and terminology, but in general terms.

Revenue less cost of sales = gross profit

- This is often referred to as the contribution, as this figure is seen as contributing towards the other costs of the business).

Gross profit less other operating costs = operating profit

Operating profit less finance costs less taxation = net profit

- This is the amount which has been generated for the shareholders of the company during the period. Net profit can be used to pay a dividend, or it can be retained in the reserves of the company; in either case, it belongs to the shareholders.

NED checklist

- Is an income statement provided as part of the management information on a regular basis?
- Does the financial director regularly discuss the core aspects of the income statement, making it clear where there have been accounting adjustments, and commenting on any unusual movements or trends?
- Do the NEDs regularly discuss the income statement provided to monitor the performance of the company?

Financial Reporting Council

Introduction

The Financial Reporting Council (FRC) is currently an independent regulator in the UK. In structure, it is a company limited by guarantee and is funded by the audit profession and other groups who are required to contribute for the benefit of receiving FRC regulation. As the FRC evolved, it gathered together six different operating bodies under one banner:

- Accounting Standards Board
- Financial Reporting Review Panel
- Accountancy and Actuarial Discipline Board
- Professional Oversight Board
- Auditing Practices Board
- Board for Actuarial Standards.

The FRC describes its own role as follows:

- 'The FRC's mission is to promote transparency and integrity in business. These are cornerstones to generating public trust and attracting investment in sustainable, successful companies that provide jobs, create prosperity and generate economic growth.'
- 'We do this by regulating accountants, auditors and actuaries, and by operating the UK's corporate governance system.'
- 'We encourage directors of companies to fulfil their responsibilities to wider society as well as their company's shareholders.'
- 'We implement standards…'
- 'To deliver our mission we must also be transparent and act with integrity.'

Despite the FRC having accumulated an increasing breadth of oversight, this has often been without real authority or power to enforce change.

Corporate failures have continued, concern over effective auditing continues and there is cyclical concern about the appropriateness of pay levels for the highest paid directors (and others further down the scale).

There are serious questions from many sides about the efficacy of audit and financial oversight. These areas were epitomised in 2018 by the failures of Carillion and BHS, the accounting issues at Patisserie Valerie, and the increase of shareholder revolts against executive remuneration.

As a result of this, BEIS established three separate reviews to consider a better way forward for corporate oversight and audit. The first of these to report was led by John Kingman. His remit was to review the work and regulation of the FRC, with the view of evolving a new regulator which would be 'a beacon for the best in governance, transparency, and independence'.

The major change being proposed by the Kingman Review is the replacement of the FRC with a new regulator to be known as the Audit, Reporting and Governance Authority (ARGA). The new regulator is to be directly accountable to the UK Parliament through BEIS and will have significant powers and oversight.

Kingman's views of the current state of the FRC is best summarised in words from his report:

> … an institution constructed in a different era – a rather ramshackle house, cobbled together with all sorts of extensions over time. The house is – just – serviceable, up to a point, but it leaks and creaks, sometimes badly. The inhabitants of the house have sought to patch and mend. But in the end, the house is built on weak foundations. It is time to build a new house.

NED checklist

- Are you, as a NED, aware of the plethora of publications available to download from the FRC website to help in the performance of your role? Although many of the publications are required reading for listed company NEDs they bring a balance and challenge to the role of a NED in any type and size of organisation.
- What are the implications for your company of a change from voluntary regulation (FRC) to statutory regulation (ARGA)?
- Are your external auditors fit for purpose? Is there a conflict in the work that they undertake for you between audit work and non-audit work?
- As a NED, if challenged by a regulator, could you defend the approach of your company and its directors to the oversight, mitigation and control of risk within the organisation, from both an internal and an external audit perspective?
- Ensure that you have a means of keeping up to date with the latest changes in the oversight and regulation of companies and that you and your fellow directors consider the implication for your company on a regular basis.

Further information

- Checklist: Audit Reporting and Governance Authority, page 25.
- Independent Review of the Financial Reporting Council (Kingman Review) 2018. Available at: assets.publishing.service.gov.uk/government/uploads/system/uploads/attachment_data/file/767387/frc-independent-review-final-report.pdf.

GAAP

Introduction

GAAP is an acronym for Generally Accepted Accounting Principles.

This is a common set of accepted accounting principles, standards and procedures that companies and accountants are expected to follow when compiling their statutory financial statements. While technically referring to the year-end public financial statements, in general terms, the majority of organisations will follow the GAAP approach in maintaining and completing their regular day-to-day, week-to-week, month-to-month management accounting.

The purpose of a GAAP approach is to improve the clarity and comparability of financial statements from different companies and ensure a consistency from year-to-year within and between companies.

In reality, in the environment of 'true and fair accounting', there is still plenty of scope for interpretation and variation from a perceived accepted median. The desire for clarity and transparency is equally obfuscated by the existence of two similar but different concepts of GAAP – US GAAP and UK GAAP. This is further confused by the rapid spread and required adoption of International Financial Reporting Standards (IFRS). Larger companies will often, therefore, report GAAP, non-GAAP and IFRS figures as three different perspectives of the same underlying performance.

All these approaches are similar at their core, but there are a range of substantive and material differences.

NED checklist

- Are you clear which accounting principles are followed by your company and why?
- If the annual reports show alternative figures for GAAP and IFRS, are you clear on where the differences are and why?
- Are the accounting principles which have been adopted reflected in the financial statements and information that is received by directors?

- Do the year-end financial statements reflect the information and explanations provided to the directors during the year?
- Do you have sufficient confidence and understanding of the finances and financial reports of the company for the annual financial statements to be signed in your name as a director? Although one named director will sign the accounts, it is on behalf of each of the other directors.

GDPR

Introduction

The General Data Protection Regulation (GDPR) came into effect on 25 May 2018 and was incorporated into the updated Data Protection Act 2018. Although originating within the European Union, it builds upon existing UK data protection law to strengthen the protection of an individual's personal data. It requires that the personal data of every UK citizen, especially if sensitive, must be protected however and wherever it is stored.

In essence, data protection is the fair and proper use of information about people. It is part of the fundamental right to privacy and requires the building of trust between people and organisations. Data protection is about treating people fairly and openly, recognising their right to have control over their own identity and their interactions with others and striking a balance with the wider interests of society.

Most businesses are classed as data controllers through their holding of:

- employee records;
- customer databases; and
- technical data such as IP addresses, smartphone device IDs or location information when linked to an individual.

Records held in manual filing systems fall under the regulations as well as computerised records.

Fines for non-compliance can be substantial with a maximum fine of up to 4% of annual turnover for the worst offenders. GDPR falls under the oversight of the Information Commissioner's Office and their ethos is to work with businesses to improve compliance rather than to seek to levy fines.

Directors have a duty to ensure that their organisation is compliant with GDPR.

NED checklist

- Have the board of directors received assurance that the business is GDPR compliant? This should feature annually within a board's agenda.
- Does the business need to appoint, or has it already appointed, a data protection officer? If not, who within the organisation has ongoing oversight of the control of data under GDPR?
- Have the implications and the requirements of GDPR been explained and training given to all relevant people within the organisation?
- As a NED, have you reviewed the GDPR procedures from an objective outsider perspective?

Procedure

- Check that the relevant executive employee has ensured that:
  - all personal data is collected and handled in a lawful, fair and transparent manner;
  - personal data is only collected for specified, explicit and legitimate purposes;
  - the personal data collected is adequate, relevant and limited to only what is necessary for the purpose of processing;
  - personal data is retained no longer than necessary; and
  - all personal data retained within the organisation is appropriately secured.

Further information

- Information Commissioner's Office. Available at: www.ico.org.uk

Gearing – debt versus equity

Introduction

Gearing is a term that is often used when directors, the media and others are discussing the financial structure of a company. It is also a term that is frequently misused and has gathered a plethora of meanings.

This brief discussion seeks to redress the balance and turn the term 'gearing' to its correct context.

It is important for a NED and any director or senior manager to understand the financial infrastructure of the organisation where they are serving and to be able to bring sometimes complex concepts back to a simple base point.

At its simplest, gearing describes the relationship that exists in the financing of a company between:

- Equity – funds provided by the shareholders; and
- Debt – funds provided by banks and other lenders of finance.

A higher geared company is funded by more debt than equity.

A lower geared company is funded by more equity than debt.

The terms, however, are relative and only relevant as a point of comparison.

The importance of gearing is therefore the cost to the company (tangible and intangible) that is associated with each type of financing. In general, the cost of equity will be higher than the cost of debt.

Equity

- Shareholders are entitled to a proportionate share of any dividend paid, if sufficient post-tax profits have been made – either in the current year or profits retained from a previous year.
- Companies do not have to pay a dividend; the level of appropriate dividend is proposed by the directors each year.

- Unless a company is repurchasing its own shares, if a shareholder wishes to receive a repayment of their original capital investment into a share they will need to find a buyer for that share – easy for a listed company share, but more difficult for a private company share. At this point of sale, the shareholder will make a capital gain or loss on their investment.

Debt

Lenders of debt finance will generally have a formal loan agreement with the lender requiring the company to pay interest at a pre-determined rate and on predetermined dates, together with a repayment schedule for the repayment of the loan capital. As well as fixed-rate loans, some lenders may offer variable rate loans whereby the interest payable may be changed on a periodic basis over the period of the loan.

Thus, in most cases it is clear that the tangible liquidity cost of debt funding (outflow of cash from the business) is predetermined and fixed at the time of borrowing. Non-payment will place the company in default and could be grounds for an insolvency action.

- Debt funding will always require a tangible cash outflow from a company.
- Equity funding will only require a tangible cash outflow if sufficient post-tax profits have been generated.

However, equity finance plays a far more important intangible role in the financing.

- Shareholders in a private company are investing for the long term and are likely to take a long-term interest in the fortunes of the company.
- Shareholders in a listed company will be investing for a range of different reasons and with different levels of expectation. There is never any demand for a repayment of capital. However, the ability of the company to pay a dividend or otherwise is likely to impact the desire to buy or sell in the company and hence affect the share price which, in turn, will affect the wider reputation of the company with banks, customers, suppliers and other stakeholders.

The accounting calculation to determine the relative cost of debt and equity funding is known as the 'weighted cost of capital'.

There is no correct holistic solution as to the optimal means of funding the long-term infrastructure of a company. Each company needs to determine the appropriate mix at different times in its evolution.

NED checklist

- What is the long-term financial structure of the company?

- Would you class your company as high or low-geared? What are you comparing this to?
- How often is the long-term funding of the business discussed at the board? Actual and optimal?
- As a director the real significance is the level of potential cash outflow, and hence the ongoing liquidity of the company. Is your level of gearing likely to lead you towards insolvency?
- Be certain when you talk about gearing in your company that you are absolutely clear as to which figures are being included in the calculation in a consistent and comparative manner, and their relevance.

Notes

- The confusion around the term gearing arises from what is included by different companies, accountants, analysts and journalist in their meaning of equity and debt.
- Equity can include share capital, share premium, asset revaluations, and retained and undistributed profits from previous years. It will also be adjusted for certain IFRS recalculations such as foreign currency revaluations.
- Debt can include long-term finance funding, short-term finance funding, an offset of short-term cash assets against both short and/or long-term finance funding, and other variations.

General duties, accountabilities and obligations

Introduction

The role of a director of a company brings with it a wide and varied number of duties, accountabilities and obligations. The following checklist is not necessarily exclusive but includes the majority of areas that a director needs to be aware of. Further comment on many of these areas can be found in this book.

NED checklist

- Statutory duties of a director:
  - Duty one: to act in accordance with the constitution of the company.
  - Duty two: to promote the success of the company.
  - Duty three: to exercise independent judgement.
  - Duty four: to exercise reasonable care, skill and diligence.
  - Duty five: to avoid conflicts of interest.
  - Duty six: to not accept benefits from third parties.
  - Duty seven: to declare any interest if a proposed transaction or arrangement.
- Statutory financial duties:
  - Ensure the company keeps adequate financial records, sufficient to disclose with reasonable accuracy the financial position of the company and its transactions.
  - Only approve the accounts of the company when satisfied that they give a 'true and fair' view of the assets, liabilities, financial position and profit or loss of the company.
  - Disclose transactions undertaken between the company and the directors.
  - Have sight of and approve the annual directors' report.

  - Have sight of and approve the annual strategic report, required from all except small companies, be aware of the expectations from this report, in particular the new section 172 reporting requirements with regard to stakeholder awareness.
  - Maintain an awareness of the going concern stability of the company. It is illegal to continue to trade whilst insolvent, and directors will be held liable for this.
- Governance expectations:
  - Listed company: be aware of the Listing Rules expectations with regard to the UK Corporate Governance Code 2018.
  - Large company: be aware of the expectations under the Companies Act and the alignment with the Wates Governance Principles for Large Private Companies.
- Additional statutory and other duties and expectations:
  - Ensure that all statutory returns are filed in a timely manner.
  - Ensure that the annual report and accounts are filed on time.
  - Maintain appropriate communication with shareholders.
  - Maintain minutes of directors' meeting and associated documents for 10 years.
  - Be aware of and comply with employment laws.
  - Be aware of and comply with health and dafety regulations; make sure the company has a clear and up-to-date health and safety policy.
  - Ensure that all taxes, including value-added tax (VAT) and pay as you earn (PAYE)/national insurance (NI) contributions are paid on time.
  - Ensure that the company is compliant with the GDPR.
  - Maintain an awareness of the timely settlement of the liabilities of the company.
  - Have an awareness of the expectations of the Corporate Manslaughter Act 2007.
  - Have an awareness of the expectations of the Bribery Act 2010.
  - Have an awareness of the expectations of the Modern Slavery Act 2015.

Going concern

Introduction

Going concern is the bedrock of financial prudence and a fundamental requirement for any organisation. Directors are required to ensure that organisations meet this expectation and auditors are required to audit this. It has been an accepted practice within accounting for many years and has generally been an accepted sign-off point for organisational viability and responsibility. Although this does not mean it has to be profit making, 'going concern' is a concept which implies viability for each individual organisation within its own expected operating parameters.

Going concern, as a core accounting assumption, is the assurance from the directors of a company that the entity can recognise how its liabilities will be funded or underpinned by its assets for the foreseeable future.

It is a recognised part of any required audit process, where a confirmation is sought that the figures have been prepared on a 'going concern' basis. The recognised assets are seen as the basis of future delivery, with an underlying presumption that there is no requirement (for the foreseeable future) to liquidate those assets on an emergency basis, or to substantively change the operational business model.

A problem faced by accountants and others is the timescale of the perception of 'foreseeable' alongside the time structure of the organisation. Financial statements are required to be prepared, at a fixed balance-sheet date, on a going concern basis with the organisation being viewed as continuing in business for the foreseeable future.

The word 'foreseeable' is not defined within international accounting standards (IAS) but the foreseeable future is presumed to be a period of 12 months from the organisation's reporting date.

NED checklist

- Be aware of the company's basis for assessing going concern.
- Have a knowledge of and a confidence in the figures on the balance sheet representing the assets and liabilities of the company.

- Check the wording of the going concern statement ascribed to the directors in the annual report and accounts.
- Discuss going concern with the external auditors of the company, understand their interrogation process, the wording of their statement and any concerns that they might hold.
- Be aware of the role of the external auditors of the company in terms of their assessment and any concerns raised regarding the going-concern concept.
- Be prepared to be sceptical.

Procedure

- Until 2014, the reporting of going concern within an organisation was relatively straightforward and formulaic:
  - the directors of the company were required under statute to ensure that the organisation was able to meet its liabilities;
  - the external auditors of the organisation were required to assess that a correct and appropriate matching of assets and liabilities underpinned the immediate viability of the company (the foreseeable future); and
  - the external auditors were required to include in their audit report a statement to the fact that the audit had been carried out on the organisation on a going concern basis and that, as external auditors, they had been satisfied that the organisation was indeed a going concern.
- Following the 2007/2008 banking and liquidity crisis, the FRC commissioned an inquiry, led by Lord Sharman under the title 'Going Concern and Liquidity Risks: Lessons for companies and auditors'. The final report and recommendations of this inquiry recognised that the taking of 'sensible' risk is critical to organisational growth and the continuance of wider economic activity. The recommendations from the inquiry suggested that directors should:
  - ensure that the going concern assessment process, risks, conclusions and statement are transparent;
  - establish a common understanding of purpose, thresholds and what constitutes a going concern within the organisation and how it might differ from other organisations;
  - integrate the going concern assessment with business planning and risk management; and
  - require the external auditor to include in their audit report an explicit statement concerning the robustness with which the directors had carried out their going concern assessment, together with any resultant recommendations.

Requirements

- It is a recognised part of any required audit process where a confirmation is sought that the figures have been prepared on a 'going concern' basis.
- The recognised assets are seen as the basis of future delivery, with an underlying presumption that there is no requirement (for the foreseeable future) to liquidate those assets on an emergency basis, or to substantively change the operational business model.
- A problem faced by accountants and others is the timescale of the perception of 'foreseeable' alongside the time structure of the organisation. Financial statements are required to be prepared, at a fixed balance-sheet date, on a going concern basis with the organisation being viewed as continuing in business for the foreseeable future.
- The word 'foreseeable' is not defined within international accounting standards (IAS) but the foreseeable future is presumed to be a period of 12 months from the organisation's reporting date.

Notes

- The concept of going concern tends to focus on the current and future levels of assets over liabilities from a shareholder wealth perspective. The reality for many organisations is that the going concern concept is more closely related to the wider stakeholder relationships and hence requires a more detailed consideration, and alignment with concepts of longer-term viability.

Further information

- See the FRC website for a variety of guidance on going concern. Available at: www.frc.org.uk
- Sharman enquiry report: 'Going Concern and Liquidity Risks: Lessons for companies and auditors'.

Health and safety

Introduction

Directors of a business have a fundamental role in ensuring that adequate and appropriate health and safety protection and control exists for the employees of the business and for any members of the public who may be affected by the activities of the business.

The Health and Safety at Work etc Act 1974 places a duty of care on the organisation as an employer, and on the directors of the company as the individuals with oversight of the organisation.

Directors have a collective and individual responsibility for health and safety within the business. One or more directors can be held personally liable when and if these duties are deemed to have been breached.

NED checklist

- What are the governance, regulation and reporting requirements applicable to your company in relation to risk management, which includes health and safety?
- Is health and safety regularly considered by the directors?
  - No: make sure it is on the next board agenda.
  - Yes: do you, as a company, take all appropriate action to protect the company and its employees?
- Are employees aware of the health and safety policy? How? Do you regularly (annually, semi-annually) remind people about the requirements of the policy and the implications of getting it wrong?
- Are you aware of, and have you read the health and safety policy?
- Is health and safety behaviour included in your code of ethics?
- How do you monitor the behaviour of your employees in this regard? As directors, you need to be able to demonstrate that you have taken all reasonable steps to protect the health and safety of your employees.
- In the case of a serious incident, who will lead the company's external communication with media and other interested parties?

Procedure

- Health and safety policy and culture should be led from the top by the board of directors.
- Directors must assure themselves that health and safety regulations are complied with and that a policy is in place, commensurate with the size, complexity and activities of the organisation.
- Directors must satisfy themselves that all employees of the business, including senior managers, have ready access to the health and safety policy and that their awareness and training is refreshed as required by the size, complexity and activities of the organisation.
- Directors must ensure that appropriate communication channels exist to enable regular information on health and safety incidents, and that an escalation process exists for directors to be rapidly informed of any serious incidents.
- Directors should have an agreed communication policy for comments to the media or other external stakeholders if a serious incident occurs. It is advisable and usual to have one or two specifically trained people in place to handle such external communications.

Notes

- The Corporate Manslaughter and Corporate Homicide Act 2007 allows for the prosecution of the organisation, together with its directors and senior management, for a breach of the duty of care to the organisation's employees or members of the public, which results in death. The maximum penalty for proven corporate manslaughter is an unlimited fine together with a potential publicity order requiring the organisation to publish the details of its conviction and fine.

Independent non-executive directors

Introduction

The expectation that a board of directors will contain a majority of independent non-executive directors (INEDs) has evolved over the past 30 years to the point where the UK Corporate Governance Code 2018 states in Principle G:

> The board should include an appropriate combination of executive and non-executive (and, in particular, independent non-executive) directors, such that no one individual or small group of individuals dominates the board's decision making.

Provision 11 of the UK Code goes further:

> At least half the board, excluding the chair, should be non-executive directors whom the board considers to be independent.

NED checklist

- Are you classed as an INED? If so, is this appropriate and correct?
- Do you have a sufficient diversity of INEDs and independence of thinking around the board table?
- Is independent challenge encouraged from all the NEDs, whether an INED or not?
- If required, do you meet the independence expectations of the UK Code?

Procedure

- In law, an INED is no different to a NED or any other director.
- The procedure for formal appointment and registration at Companies House is therefore no different for any director.
- The point of differentiation should be driven by the nomination committee when defining the succession requirements for the board and ensuring an appropriate list of potential directors are considered

for recruitment. The need for independence must be recognised as a core attribute at this stage.

Requirements

- The approach to effective governance that is recommended within the UK Code goes far further and is looking for an actual and perceived level of genuine independence from the company.
- Provision 9: 'The chair should be independent on appointment when assessed against the circumstances set out in Provision 10.'
- Provision 10: The board should identify in the annual report each non-executive director it considers to be independent. Circumstances which are likely to impair, or could appear to impair, a non-executive director's independence include, but are not limited to, whether a director:
  - is or has been an employee of the company or group within the last five years;
  - has, or has had within the last three years, a material business relationship with the company, either directly or as a partner, shareholder, director or senior employee of a body that has such a relationship with the company;
  - has received or receives additional remuneration from the company apart from a director's fee, participates in the company's share option or a performance-related pay scheme, or is a member of the company's pension scheme;
  - has close family ties with any of the company's advisers, directors or senior employees;
  - holds cross-directorships or has significant links with other directors through involvement in other companies or bodies;
  - represents a significant shareholder; or
  - has served on the board for more than nine years from the date of their first appointment.
- Where any of these or other relevant circumstances apply, and the board nonetheless considers that the non-executive director is independent, a clear explanation should be provided.

Notes

- What is really meant by independence?
- Section 173 of CA2006 states 'a director of a company must exercise independent judgement'. That underpins the concept of independence, that each director acts as an individual and cannot place reliance or blame on the other directors.

- The intent of this duty is to remind each director that they are required to exercise their own independent judgement for each decision being made, and to feel confident to express their own views on any particular matter being addressed by the board. It does not mean that a NED has to be an INED.

Further information

- FRC: UK Corporate Governance Code (2018). Available at https://www.frc.org.uk/getattachment/88bd8c45-50ea-4841-95b0-d2f4f48069a2/2018-UK-Corporate-Governance-Code-FINAL.pdf

Induction programme

Introduction

In the early days of joining a board of directors, it is important for a NED to participate in a structured induction programme.

This should be tailored to the needs of the individual and designed, proportionate with the size and complexity of the business, to introduce and explain the culture, finances, risks, reporting, procedures, operational activities, and other pertinent matters relating to the business. This process may take 12 months in order to cover a full board cycle.

This will enable the new director to participate in as full a manner as early as possible in the governance of the business and other associated NED duties and expectations.

NED checklist

- Does a NED induction programme exist? Who is responsible for the co-ordination and design of this?
- Have you participated fully in such a programme?
- Do you have sufficient knowledge of all required aspects of the business to enable me to fulfil my role as a NED?
- What part should you play in ensuring that an appropriate induction programme exists for future NEDs?

Procedure

- The provision of an appropriate induction programme for NEDs should be overseen by the chair of the business, often in consultation with the nomination committee.
- The company secretary will often control the logistics of such an induction programme, ensuring that the new NED is aware of relevant aspects.

Requirements

- An appropriately structured NED induction programme should include as a minimum:
  - Provision of relevant past board papers, including previous board evaluations. In reality many directors will have requested sight of such documentation as part of their own due diligence process before accepting the role of NED.
  - Time should be spent with other NEDs and with the key executive directors of the business.
  - Time should also be spent with non-managerial members of the workforce to gain a better understanding of the way the business actually works in practice and to gain an insight into the experience and concerns of the workforce.
  - If appropriate, the induction programme should include visits to different sites and operational centres of the business.
  - Presentations by senior executives or external consultants or advisers.
  - Meetings with shareholders and other important stakeholders.
  - Attendance at conferences or formal training courses.

Further information

- The Chartered Governance Institute: guidance note, 'Induction of directors'.
- ICSA Publishing: The Non Executive Directors' Handbook, chapter 12 (2019).
- FRC: UK Corporate Governance Code (2018).
- FRC: Guidance on Board Effectiveness (2018).

Insider dealing

Introduction

Insider dealing is a criminal offence under Part V of the Criminal Justice Act 1993. The offence of insider dealing may take the following form:

- knowingly dealing in securities on the basis of inside information;
- encouraging another to engage in such dealing; and
- disclosing inside information otherwise than in the proper performance of one's employment, office or profession.

Insider dealing forms one of three offences under the EU Market Abuse Regulation (MAR), the other two being:

- unlawful disclosure – information must only be disclosed in the manner prescribed by the MAR and other statutes; and
- market manipulation – this is defined in MAR as transaction orders or behaviour which give false or misleading signals of supply, demand or price of securities and the dissemination of information which gives false or misleading signals of supply or demand or price.

Insider dealing arises when a person possesses inside information and uses that information by dealing in securities or by cancelling or changing an existing transaction in respect of securities.

Under MAR, inside information generally means information which:

- relates, directly or indirectly, to particular instruments or issuers;
- is of a precise nature;
- has not been made public; and
- if it were made public, would be likely to have a significant effect on the price of those instruments.

An offence is also committed where a person recommends that another person engages in insider dealing or induces another person to engage in insider dealing.

The essential characteristic of insider dealing consists of an unfair advantage being obtained for inside information to the detriment of third parties who are unaware of such information and, consequently, the undermining of the integrity of financial markets and investor confidence

The fact that information about a company exists but is unpublished does not itself make that information 'inside information'; the relevant criteria must also be met.

To be guilty of the offence, the information must have been obtained by the defendant as a director, employee or shareholder of the company concerned, or directly or indirectly from such a person and they must have known that the information was inside information.

The freedom of directors and certain senior employees of listed companies to deal in their securities is subject to MAR. This is necessary as it should be assumed that such senior people will have information in respect of the company of which the rest of the market may be unaware.

Consequently, MAR determines a system of periods closed for trading to try to prevent advertent or in advertent insider dealing.

NED checklist

- Ensure you are aware of the insider dealing regulations and the market abuse regulations.
- Ensure the timing of all relevant releases of information from the company where you are a NED is clear and publicised to all relevant people who might potentially be accused of insider dealing if they had access to such information.
- Ensure the security of inside information is protected and robust, such that no other person might inadvertently obtain access to that information.
- Ensure the minutes of board meetings and other appropriate board papers clearly identify the anticipated, and actual, dates of closed periods for trading in the shares of the company.

Procedure

- The Market Abuse Regulation provides for a closed trading period of 30 days prior to the announcement of the half-year year report or year-end report. Directors, officers and other senior management and people deemed as connected persons, are barred from trading in the securities of the company during that period of time.
- In the UK, most issuers release year-end preliminary results, hence the closed period will be deemed to be the 30 days prior to the announcement of the preliminary results.

Further information

- Part V of the Criminal Justice Act 1993.
- EU Market Abuse Regulation (MAR). Available at: www.icsa.org.uk/ireland/knowledge-and-guidance/legislation-and-regulation/what-constitutes-inside-information-under-the-new-market-abuse-regulation.

Institutional investors and the Stewardship Code

Introduction

The UK Stewardship Code was first issued by the FRC in 2010, revised in 2012 and then again in 2020.

It is complementary to the UK Corporate Governance Code. In the same way that the Governance Code requires directors to seek good relations with shareholders, the Stewardship Code requires institutional investors to engage constructively with the companies in which they hold shares.

Institutional investors can be defined as:

> Investment professionals who get paid to manage other people's money, including financial institutions such as banks, mutual funds, insurance companies, pension funds together with large non-financial corporations.

To a greater or lesser extent, the directors and managers of such institutional investors act in a representative role for their investors, rather than taking a personal interest for their own direct investments. They owe a duty of stewardship care to the underlying investors.

The FRC described the UK Stewardship Code 2020 as:

> A substantial and ambitious revision to the 2012 edition of the Code which takes effect from 1 January 2020. The new Code sets high expectations of those investing money on behalf of UK savers and pensioners. In particular, the new Code establishes a clear benchmark for stewardship as the responsible allocation, management and oversight of capital to create long-term value for clients and beneficiaries leading to sustainable benefits for the economy, the environment and society.

Stewardship activities include monitoring assets and service providers, engaging issuers and holding them to account on material issues, and publicly reporting on the outcome of these activities.

The main differences between the 2020 and 2012 Stewardship Code are:

- Twelve principles aimed at (i) asset managers; and (ii) asset owners and six principles aimed at service providers on an 'apply and explain' basis, compared to only seven principles aimed at all three categories, applied on a 'comply or explain' basis.

- The primary purpose of stewardship under the new Code is identified as looking after assets of beneficiaries that have been entrusted to the care of others. Furthermore, investment assets other than listed equity and investment decision-making also come under the scope of the Code.
- As well as including asset managers, the Code's focus extends to asset owners and service providers.
- Asset managers and asset owners are required to report on their specific stewardship activities and outcomes over a 12-month period, not just reporting on policies.
- Signatories of listed equity assets are required to provide greater information about their decision-making process and history.
- Signatories are required to take into account material ESG (environmental, social and governance) factors and ensure that the needs of their clients are aligned with their investment decisions.
- Signatories are required to explain their organisation's purpose, beliefs, strategy, investment and culture and how this is demonstrated through appropriate staff incentives, resourcing and governance.

NED checklist

- Are you aware of the identity and nature of the institutional investors that hold shares in our company?
- Are you satisfied with the level of communication between institutional investors?
- Do you see them as activist investors? If so, how do we ensure they are handled correctly?
- Do you have an active and mutually understanding relationship with the key representatives, directors, managers and analysts of your institutional investors?
- Do the NEDs get the opportunity to meet with the institutional investors and therefore do you have first-hand awareness of their views and opinions with regard to the company?

Procedure

- Under the 2020 Stewardship Code:
  - organisations wishing to become signatories to the 2020 Code will need to produce an annual stewardship report which explains how they have applied the Code in the last 12 months;

- the FRC will assess every year whether the report meets with its expectations so that the organisation can be included in the list of signatories;
- the first stewardship reports based on the new Code must be submitted by 31 March 2021;
- the FRC will then assess the reports and publish a first list of signatories in the third quarter of 2021. Organisations will not be tiered or ranked as before.
- Current signatories of the 2012 Code will remain as such until the first signatories list of the new 2020 Code have been published in 2021.

Notes

- The following areas were seen as drivers for change in the Stewardship Code:
  - the need to address short-termism in the markets, as challenged in the Kay Review of 2012;
  - the Financial Conduct Authority (FCA) expectation that certain financial services firms are expected to be a signatory to the Stewardship Code;
  - the evolution of workplace pension schemes;
  - the 2017 report from the Law Commission considering the need for fiduciary duty to include a consideration of long-term systemic risks such as climate change, and the need for a greater understanding of the distinction between ethical factors and ESG factors;
  - in 2017, the pensions regulator issued guidance to all pension trustees that they need to take all factors that are financially material to investment performance into account, including ESG factors;
  - a specific recommendation in 2017 from the House of Commons' Business, Energy and Industrial Strategy Committee that the UK Stewardship Code should provide more explicit expectations from signatories to the Code;
  - a range of increasing expectations from corporate governance, and the latest Companies Act 2006 reporting requirements, with s. 414 of CA2006 now requiring a 'stakeholder statement' from all companies except small companies, requiring directors to demonstrate and illustrate how they have complied with their stakeholder duties under s. 172 of CA2006;
  - the Kingman Review, published in December 2018, described the 2012 Code as 'a major and well-intentioned intervention' but 'not effective in practice'. A fundamental shift in approach was called

for, so that the Code focused on outcomes and effectiveness, not on policy statements, and if that could not be achieved serious consideration should be given to its abolition; and

- following on from the above in January 2019, a consultation was launched by the FRC on proposed amendments to the 2012 Code and a joint discussion paper that called for input on how best to encourage the institutional investment community to engage more actively in stewardship of the assets in which they invest ('Building a Regulatory Framework for Stewardship' (DP19/1)) was published by the FCA and FRC.

Further information

- FRC website: www.frc.org.uk
- FCA website: www.fca.org.uk.

Integrated reporting

Introduction

It is important to recognise that the strategic objectives of an organisation will not just be financial. The increasing importance of stakeholders is exemplified in the duties of directors (CA2006 s.172) and the reporting that is now expected in this regard from all except small companies. Directors must report how they have considered the varying expectations of their stakeholders in their decision making and formulation of strategy.

An earlier attempt to bring a wider stakeholder and environmental aspect to reporting was known as 'triple bottom line' reporting and suggested that an organisation should consider three core dimensions: social, environmental and financial. These are also known as the 'three Ps': profit, people and planet.

This has been taken to a different level by the International Integrated Reporting Council (IIRC), which actively encourages organisations to view their strategic objectives and produce their annual report and accounts in an integrated manner, ensuring that the different aspects of the report inter-relate and are not a series of isolated sections.

An integrated report is a holistic form of reporting about how an organisation's strategy, governance, performance and prospects lead to the creation of value over the short, medium and long term.

Underpinning the IIRC concept is the identification of six different forms of 'capital' within an organisation – financial, manufactured, intellectual, human, social and relationship, and natural.

NED checklist

- How have the expectations of stakeholders been considered with regard to the way you choose to report?
- Have you considered moving towards the adoption of a fully integrated reporting model such as that recommended by the IIRC?

Procedure

The IIRC approach to reporting, as illustrated in the following diagram suggests that an organisation recognises how each of the six 'capitals' feeds into its business process. This then further recognises how value has either been added or reduced to each capital as a result of the operational activities of the business.

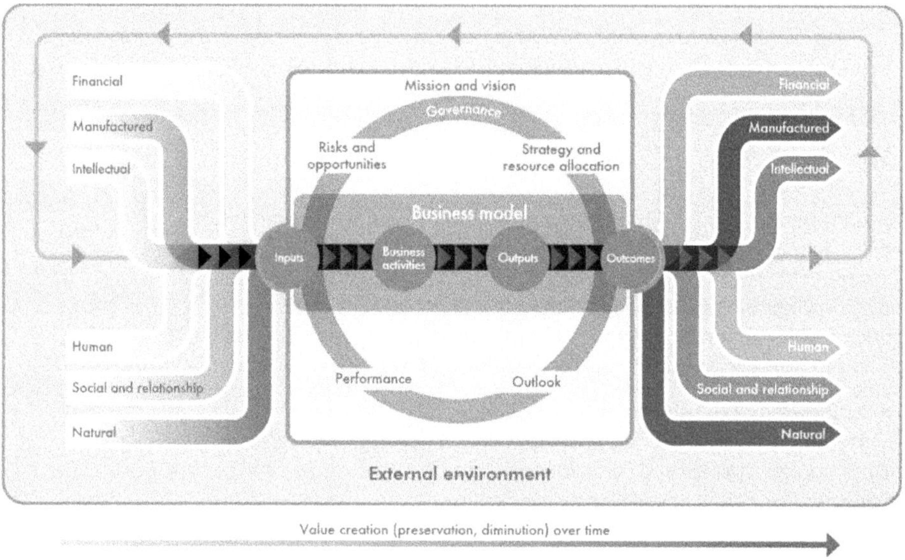

Further information

- International Integrated Reporting Council. integratedreporting.org.

Key performance indicators

Introduction

Many organisations use key performance indicators (KPIs) which are measurable values that management can use to evaluate how effectively performance and business objectives are being met.

The use of KPIs within an organisation can be both a help and a hindrance for a NED:

- They are a help if the executive directors are using relevant and dynamic KPI measures to illustrate what is actually happening within the organisation.
- They are a hindrance if the KPIs used are not reviewed or updated on a periodic basis and, lack sufficient relevance to current organisational activity and performance.

Each director of an organisation must ensure that they are in receipt of sufficient and appropriate data, information and control measures to allow them to fulfil their various duties. In this brief overview, it is sufficient to suggest that there are four core requirements to be able to use KPIs for measurement, assessment and control:

- The word KEY is fundamental: there should only ever be a closely defined set of measures which are agreed by all affected parties.
- A KPI must be based upon accurate and reliable data and information to ensure integrity and trust of the reports being generated.
- The business measurement aspect covered by a KPI must be relevant to the core strategy and objectives of the organisation.
- A realistic target should be set for each KPI in order to compare and monitor actual performance and, as a result, help to formulate future strategy in order to attain the business objectives.

NED checklist

- How do you measure performance within your organisation?
- Do you have an appropriate and sufficient set of KPIs?

- Do you understand the information being conveyed by each KPI and the data from which the KPI has been derived?
- Who has been involved in the process of formulating KPIs and what information sources have been utilised?
- Do you have a balanced and challenging set of KPIs to give the directors a deeper understanding of the business from a range of differing dimensions?
- Do you use KPIs correctly as part of your annual reporting, as required by Companies Act 2006 for all except 'small' companies? Do these reported KPIs align with the regular KPIs used in meetings of directors? If not, why not?

Procedure

- Ensure that there is a comprehensive and focused set of KPIs that are used to summarise trends and movements within the operation of the organisation.
- Irrespective of the formal reporting requirement, KPIs should cover financial and non-financial aspects of any organisation.
- Rather than just accepting the KPIs that are used within formal board meetings, dig deeper and find the KPIs that are used at different levels of the organisation. Although these might not need to form part of a regular KPI report for directors, it can be invaluable to know how people within the organisation are measuring success from their differing perspectives.

Requirements

- Section 414C of CA2006 identifies the required contents of the annual strategic report from the directors. The requirement is identified within the Act as being 'to inform members of the company and help them assess how the directors have performed their duty under section 172' (the duty to promote the success of the company, in the context of wider stakeholder awareness and considerations).
- Section 414C adds further clarity in this regard:

  (4) The review must, to the extent necessary for an understanding of the development, performance or position of the company's business, include analysis using key performance indicators, and, where appropriate, analysis using other key performance indicators, including information relating to environmental and employee matters

  (5) "key performance indicators" means factors by reference to which the development, performance or position of the company's business can be measured effectively.

Notes

- Small companies are exempt from statutory KPI reporting (and from producing a strategic report) but may wish to still include appropriate KPIs where relevant in their communications.
- Medium-sized companies are required to include financial KPIs in their statutory strategic report, but are exempted from including non-financial KPIs, unless they wish to do so.
- Large companies and all quoted companies are required to include comprehensive financial and non-financial KPIs within their annual strategic report.

Further information

- Checklist: Strategic report, page 257.

Loans to directors

Introduction

Sections 197 to 214 of CA2006 allow a company to make loans, quasi-loans (where the company reimburses a director's creditor) or other related transactions to directors.

This is provided that there has been prior approval by ordinary resolution by the members of the company. If the company's articles require a higher standard of resolution in general meeting this will override the statutory position. In order for approval to be given in a general meeting there must be full disclosure in advance by including the following information in a memorandum which explains the loan:

- the purpose of the loan transaction;
- the amount of the loan or value of the transaction; and
- the liability to which the company may be exposed under the loan or transaction.

Shareholder approval is not required under the following circumstances, which apply where loans or transactions are in respect of small amounts, if the company is in the business of lending money or funds have been made available to the director to meet expenditure for the purposes of the company:

- loans or quasi-loans up to £10,000;
- up to £15,000 for credit transactions under which the director acquires goods from the company on deferred payment terms;
- to enable a director to meet expenditure incurred for the purpose of the company's business to enable them to perform their duties. The aggregate amount outstanding must not exceed £50,000 pounds; and
- if a loan is made by a money lending company in the ordinary course of its business and on normal terms, there is no limit to the loan amount.

NED checklist

- Does the company have a policy on making loans to directors?
- Does the policy require any particular shareholder approval?
- Are loans and amounts owed by directors to the company clear and transparent within the accounts and records of the company?
- Has the company complied with any required reporting in this regard?

Notes

- One category of transaction that is distinguished from loans is where the articles allow directors to use the company funds to meet the expense of carrying out their functions as directors. When a director spends the company's money for that purpose that director is acting as an agent of the company and not as a borrower.

Longer-term viability

Introduction

The 2007/2008 banking and liquidity crisis caused the government of the day to initiate a number of commissions and enquiries to consider how better to assess organisational viability in the future. As part of this process, in early 2011, the FRC commissioned an enquiry to be led by Lord Sharman under the title 'Going Concern and Liquidity Risks: Lessons for companies and auditors'. Part of the purpose of the enquiry was an attempt to encourage all directors to consider a longer period of viability than the traditional 12-month foreseeable future that had always been linked with the going concern concept.

A separate enquiry into the dangers of short-termism in financial markets was led by Professor John Kay in 'UK Equity Markets and Long-term Decision Making'. In the report of his committee to the UK government, Professor Kay suggested:

> short-termism, or myopic behaviour, is the natural human tendency to make decisions in search of immediate gratification at the expense of future returns: decisions which we subsequently regret.

He also suggested that 'short-termism can manifest itself in hyperactivity'. The alignment of these two reports from Sharman and Kay led to the FRC bringing in a requirement for directors of companies covered by the UK Corporate Governance Code to include a 'longer-term viability statement' within their narrative reporting.

NED checklist

- Have the directors considered the appropriate time period for the assessment of longer-term viability?
- Does the assessment period realistically relate to the business model and the strategy of the organisation?
- Have you read and agreed the longer-term viability statement, remember that it is being issued in your name?

Procedure

- The longer-term viability statement is required to explain how the directors of the company

  have assessed the prospects of the company, over what period they have done so and why they consider that period to be appropriate, taking into account the company's current position and principal risks.

- The relationship between sustainability and narrative reporting implied in the longer-term viability statement requires the words in the annual report and accounts to be aligned within themselves and with the financial results. The result being that it should be possible to interpret and analyse the going-concern nature of any sustainability statement and its relative positioning and materiality within the longer-term viability of the organisation.

Requirements

- In its 2014 update of the UK Corporate Governance Code, a new provision required the inclusion in the annual report and accounts of a longer-term viability the statement. In Provision 31 of the 2018 UK Corporate Governance Code, this is expressed as:

  > Taking account of the company's current position and principal risks, the board should explain in the annual report how it has assessed the prospects of the company, over what period it has done so and why it considers that period to be appropriate. The board should state whether it has a reasonable expectation that the company will be able to continue in operation and meet its liabilities as they fall due over the period of their assessment, drawing attention to any qualifications or assumptions as necessary.

- Further guidance on the real meaning of these words was included by the FRC in its 'Guidance on Risk Management, Internal Control and Related Financial and Business Reporting' by suggesting that *'reasonable expectation does not mean certainty'*.
- With an underlying legal basis of 'true and fair', directors need to assure themselves that their confidence in the viability of the company is based upon auditable logical facts, projections and sceptical consideration of potential variance to those projections.
- The FRC recognises that 'except in rare circumstances the period of consideration for longer-term viability should be significantly longer than 12 months from the approval of the financial statements'. The appropriate period of time will be determined by the specific circumstances of each organisation.
- Directors must determine the timescale of their projections in consideration of their capital structure, their exposure to long-term

debt, the nature of their business operation, the likelihood of the continuance of their revenue stream under different circumstances, and the overall financial stability, both short and long term.

- The FRC recommends that directors consider the financial viability from two differing perspectives:
  - *Solvency*: the ability of the company to meet its financial liabilities in full.
  - *Liquidity*: the ability of the company to meet its liabilities as they fall due.

Further information

- Sharman Report: 'Going Concern and Liquidity Risks: Lessons for companies and auditors'.
- Kay Report: 'UK Equity Markets and Long-term Decision Making'.
- FRC: website guidance and UK Corporate Governance Code (2018).

Management accounting

Introduction

Management accounting refers to the internal practice of the maintenance of a company's cost accounts together with the production of appropriate reports on a periodic basis as a guide to how the company is performing.

It is distinct from financial accounting which is the production of year-end figures in line with the specific expectations of GAAP and IFRS.

An awareness of the management accounts of a company is of significance to directors. A regular review of the ongoing management accounting records will enhance the directors' ability to be confident in the financial performance and position of the company.

The structure, level of detail and nature of management accounting and management reporting is not prescribed. It is up to each company to determine an appropriate level of structure and reporting to align with its size, complexity, risk and the demands of directors. In some companies, the management accounting policy will be driven by the expectations of providers of finance (e.g. banks) or other interested and influential stakeholders.

NED checklist

- Do you receive regular management accounts in sufficient detail to enable an ongoing understanding of the financial position of the company?
- Are the reports produced in a timely, accurate and consistent manner?
- Do all the directors (including the NEDs) understand the figures, the process and the decisions and judgements that have been made to deliver a set of management accounts within any particular organisation?
- Does the management accounting information include reports on profitability, wealth and liquidity?

- Does the management accounting information enable the directors to be confident in the ongoing solvency of the company?
- When was the last time a NED raised a challenge or material question on the regular management accounting information? There is a significant risk of habit and acceptance of management accounting information developing in a board room.
- When did all the NEDs last have a one-to-one discussion with the Head of Finance and/or the Head of Management Accounts?

Procedure

- The executive directors of the company should propose a schedule of management accounting reporting dates for the financial year of the company – it would be normal for this to be monthly, but quarterly might be acceptable in certain companies.
- The board of directors should agree to this schedule, and, as far as possible board meeting dates should be set to enable challenge and discussion of recently produced management accounts.
- Directors, especially NEDs, should feel empowered to ask through the chair for any further information that they require to fully understand the finances of the company.

Materiality

Introduction

The concept of materiality is important for all directors of a company, but it is particularly important for NEDs to have an understanding of the implications of materiality.

Materiality relates to the significance of transactions, amounts, balances, and errors contained within the finances and accounting of an organisation and its related reporting.

Materiality defines the level or point at which a quantifiable amount (this could be either monetary or volume) becomes significant or relevant to the users or reviewers of such data or information.

It is important for a board of directors, and for all other stakeholder users of financial information, to have trust and confidence that financial information is complete in all material respects to enable presentation and consideration of a 'true and fair' view of the profitability, liquidity and wealth of an organisation.

Materiality will therefore, by its nature, differ within each organisation. The relevance and materiality of any figure, or set of figures, can only be judged when placed in the context of other figures. Materiality is always relative to the size and particular circumstances of any individual entity.

An external audit will be based around materiality levels; the auditor process looking for and focusing on figures that exceed the materiality thresholds. The appropriate levels of materiality should be, discussed, understood and agreed by the audit committee and subsequently all directors.

NED checklist

- Is materiality understood by board members?
- Do you have a clear view of the core financial drivers, the relevant levels of materiality, and the deviation parameters which could raise the risk levels?
- Does the audit committee discuss and agree the level of materiality with the external auditors??

- Are materiality levels reviewed each year to reflect the changing nature of the operation and the business environment?
- Is there a clarity and distinction between materiality with regard to profitability, liquidity and balance-sheet drivers?

Requirements

Materiality is underpinned by the core accounting concepts of:

- Relevance: material information needs to include all associated dimensions to ensure that users and decision makers are appropriately focused. A useful test is to consider the depth and breadth of the potential information and influences.
- Reliability: material information needs to be based on a logical and trusted audit trail. This might, of course, include 'fair' judgements that have been made to derive the material information, so the maker(s) of those judgements must be included within the relevant audit trail.
- Completeness: material information must be set within the appropriate context. If it represents the 'whole picture' then the underpinning data must be transparent. If it represents partial information then the 'whole picture' must be transparent.

Matters reserved for the board

Introduction

As part of its effective governance of a business, a board of directors must delegate day-to-day responsibility for the operation of the business to the executive management and directors. However, in any company there are a number of matters which are required to be decided by the board of directors as a whole, in the best interests of the company and of its shareholders.

It is good practice for a board of directors to maintain a formal schedule of matters that are specifically reserved for the board's decision. Often the annual report will contain a high-level statement of which types of decisions are taken by the board and which are delegated to management.

NED checklist

- Does the company have a specific document for matters reserved for the board?
- If yes, is it up-to-date and appropriate?
- If no, the need for it or otherwise should be reconsidered on at least an annual basis by the board of directors as a whole.

Requirements

- The 2018 UK Corporate Governance Code makes no specific requirement for a board of directors to maintain a 'matters reserved' document. However, it is still deemed to be good practice for this to be part of the board documents.
- The contents of a matters reserved schedule are likely to include but will not be restricted to the following – each company needs to determine the optimal mixture for its particular circumstances.
  - Strategy and management: the board has responsibility for the overall leadership of the company and the setting of the company's values, standards and strategic aims and objectives.

- Structure and capital: any change in the financial infrastructure of the business will usually need formalising by the board of directors. This is likely to include changes to banking arrangements.
- Financial reporting and control: the annual and interim report and accounts, together with its associated narrative reporting, is issued by the directors of the company and will therefore require a formal board decision.
- Internal control: the board must ensure that the assets of the business and the effectiveness of its operation are subject to robust and appropriate internal control systems.
- Contracts: the directors will usually maintain a level above which any contractual commitment of the company requires approval by the board of directors.
- Communication: the directors will normally be responsible for ensuring dialogue and regulatory communication with shareholders and external press communications of matters decided by the board.
- Board membership and appointments are normally within the control of the directors, subject to the constitution of the company.
- Remuneration of directors and senior management is a matter for the directors, and the remuneration committee.
- Delegation of authority: clearly defined roles, delegation of authorities, the establishment of committees and the two-way information and communication should be decided by the board.
- Corporate governance and the setting and oversight of corporate culture must stem from the top of the organisation and therefore needs to form part of the directors' deliberation of strategy and structure.
- Policies and other: a list of key policies and codes that are the responsibility of the board should be set out, plus any other key areas requiring board level decisions, such as political donations, pensions, insurances, key advisers and the matters reserved for the board schedule.

Further information

- The Chartered Governance Institute: nuidance note, 'Matters reserved for the board'.

Media and communication

Introduction

Today's media-driven world of instant communication requires a board of directors to have a firm set of principles about who is and who is not permitted to speak to the media. It is also important to define the circumstances under which any media comment can and/or must be made, and by whom.

This is not a statutory requirement, although the impact of good or bad communication might impact upon the stakeholder duties and expectations of CA2006 (s. 172 in particular) and therefore potentially might place the directors of the company at risk of action.

NED checklist

- Is there a clear policy on who is authorised to talk to the media, and under what circumstances?
- When was this last discussed at a board meeting?
- When did the authorise person (or people) last receive appropriate professional media training?
- Is there an established escalation policy to warn directors and senior managers of a potential media interest in the affairs of the company?

Procedure

- The board should agree who is the lead media spokesperson for the company, and who should deputise in the absence of that person:
  - under normal ongoing circumstances; and
  - in the case of emergency, risk, damage or disaster.
- The lead communicator will often be the chair or CEO, and the deputy will often be one of the other directors of the organisation.

- Each such person should receive appropriate professional media training to ensure that they are capable of dealing with an inquisitive, investigative and probing journalist.
- The board should establish a clear policy in the regard and publish it within the organisation.
- The company handbook, or code of ethics, that is applicable to and distributed to each employee should make it clear that they are not entitled under any circumstances to speak on behalf of the company, or to give positive or negative comments to the media on any aspect of the company's activities, practice or culture. Such behaviour in contravention of the company's rules is often classed as a gross misconduct offence.
- If the directors believe that a corporate announcement is likely to attract media interest, it is good practice to remind employees of the 'no comment' policy, and where they should direct any media enquiries or approaches that are made.

Memorandum of association

Introduction

The memorandum of association (memorandum) forms part of the constitution documents of a company, and therefore part of the structure authorised and approved by the shareholders, the member of the company.

Until October 2009, a memorandum contained an 'objects' clause which determined and restricted the activities of the company and the authority of the directors. Anything undertaken by the directors which was outside these 'objects' was viewed as *ultra vires*, (beyond the authorised powers), and therefore potentially placed the directors in breach of their duty and their authority.

In October 2009 the changes brought about through the Companies Act 2006 came into law. The memorandum continues to exist, but it is only a statement confirming the initial member (subscriber) structure of a company, and that each member has agreed to take at least one share.

Unless the articles of association (articles) restrict the activities of the company or its directors, they are now free to do anything lawful. An example of such a restriction might be a charity whereby the articles would restrict the directors to only undertake activities that have a charitable purpose – the only difference either side of October 2009 being that since that date the restriction would appear in the articles.

NED checklist

- If the company was formed after October 2009, do the articles contain any restrictions that otherwise would have appeared in the memorandum?
- If the company was formed before October 2009, have the articles been rewritten to replace any requirements or expectations originally contained in the memorandum?
- Have you seen and read the articles, and if applicable the memorandum for your company?

- As mentioned in the notes below, do the articles contain any restrictions by default?
- Is your constitution clear, comprehensible and written in modern English?

Notes

- The 'objects clause' of a company formed before October 2009 will be deemed to have been automatically transferred from the memorandum to the articles. It is worth noting that such a transferred clause may not appear within the version of the articles held on file at Companies House. However, the original objects will still be deemed to exist and therefore act as a restriction on the company and its directors.
- Even when there is no restriction, directors are required to follow the statutory duties of directors and, in particular, to always 'promote the success of the company for the benefit of its members as a whole' (CA2006 s.172).

Minutes

Introduction

Directors are required to ensure that minutes are kept of all directors, shareholders and class meetings, together with members resolutions approved otherwise than at a general or class meeting, and that these such minutes are kept in an appropriate manner.

Minutes of meetings should be crafted carefully as they provide audit trail evidence of key decisions made by those present at meetings.

They are admissible in a court of law as evidence, it is therefore advisable to ensure that not just the decision is minuted but the thinking and intent behind that decision. With particular regard to s. 172 of CA2006, this might prove invaluable evidence in demonstrating how the directors of a company have considered the wider stakeholder implications alongside promotion of the success of the business for the shareholders.

NED checklist

- Minutes should state the name of the company, the place, date and time of the meeting.
- The minutes should include either a statement that a quorum was present or a list of attendees.
- The minutes should record decisions reached by the meeting together with sufficient detail of the discussions to enable the intent of the meeting to be perceived.
- Any specific disagreement by a director against a particular resolution or course of action should be recorded, and if that director so wishes their name should be clearly aligned with that disagreement.

Procedure

- The minutes of the meeting are usually taken by the company secretary or another suitably qualified person.

- Draft minutes are often then circulated to those who attended the meeting for comment. It is important at this stage that the minutes are not changed to reflect what a person had intended to say rather than what they actually did say.
- Often the chair of the meeting is required to sign the agreed minutes at the next meeting, although this is not strictly a requirement in law. However, signed minutes do provide confirmed evidence of discussions and decisions made.

Notes

- Remember that minutes of a meeting should always be a record of decisions taken at the meeting, the intent of the meeting with regard to those decisions, and an accurate record of discussions and challenge within the meeting.
- Unless required for a particular purpose, such as minutes of a parliamentary session, minutes should not be a verbatim record of the meeting.
- Minutes of directors' and shareholders' meetings must be kept for at least 10 years from the date of the meeting.

Further information

- The Chartered Governance Institute: guidance note 'Effective minute taking'.

Modern Slavery Act 2015

Introduction

The Modern Slavery Act 2015 aims to prevent the crimes of slavery and/or human trafficking.

The Act requires businesses to take steps to ensure that such crimes do not take place within their own organisation or within their supply chains.

Section 54 requires the directors of commercial organisations to provide a transparent report and statement on the steps that are taken to prevent modern slavery. A commercial organisation is defined in the Act as a partnership or corporate body which:

- supplies goods or services;
- carries on all or part of its business in the UK; and
- has an annual turnover of at least £36 million.

NED checklist

- Have the implications of the Modern Slavery Act been considered by the directors?
  - No: make sure it is on the next board agenda.
  - Yes: have you, as a company, taken appropriate action to protect the company and its employees from action under this Act?
- How do you monitor the behaviour of your suppliers and your employees in this regard? As directors, you need to be able to demonstrate that you have taken all reasonable steps to prevent contravention of this Act.
- Are employees aware of the implications of this Act? How? Do you regularly (annually, semi-annually) remind people about the Act and its implications and provide training?
- Have you updated company polies to reflect the Modern Slavery Act 2015?

- Are you required to make a statement on your approach to modern slavery and our compliance with the Act?
- Is your statement on modern slavery included in your annual report and accounts, and on your website?
- Is your statement on modern slavery clear, transparent, and approved by the board of directors?

Requirements

- Section 54 of the Act recommends that a commercial organisation should include the following in a modern slavery statement.
  - A description of the organisation's structure, business and supply chains.
  - Policies adopted in relation to slavery and human trafficking.
  - Due diligence processes taken.
  - How the organisation ensures that slavery and human trafficking is not taking place within its business or supply chains – including the use of KPIs if appropriate.
  - Areas of the business that are at risk of slavery or human trafficking.
  - Training that is delivered to the employees of the business.

Notes

- A commercial organisation, as defined under the Act, does not have to be based in the UK for the Act to apply. It is equally applicable to a foreign entity that carries on at least part of its business in the UK.

Further information

- Modern Slavery Act 2015. Available at: http://www.legislation.gov.uk/ukpga/2015/30/contents/enacted

Narrative reporting

Introduction

The Companies Act 2006 introduced an alignment between the duties of a director (s. 172) and the expectations of narrative reporting (originally s. 417, now s. 414). Previously, the type and style of reporting had largely been at the behest of the organisation; now there is a legal expectation, which increasingly has been enhanced by the wider stakeholder expectations aligned with the growth of an ESG focus.

The concept of narrative reporting suggests that we have a story of some sort that needs to be told. We need to be very clear about the challenge that is involved in the compilation of the narrative report of a year in the life of an organisation. It must not just be bland words to accompany the figures.

The principles behind narrative reporting, at a director level, tend to be focused on a narrative report that accompanies the year-end financial reports. However, as a NED, it is equally important to challenge the narrative report that accompanies the regular reporting to the board and that is seen within the company. The same questions below apply and it is often only the NED who will raise the challenge as to the real meaning and intent.

The Financial Reporting Council (FRC) has made several attempts to temper the reporting enthusiasm, recognising the inordinate growth in the size and complexity of reporting. Much of this reporting is diametrically opposed to the underlying desire of shareholders, investors and regulators for increased transparency.

The average length of a FTSE350 company report is now 180 pages, so the questions must be asked. Who, other than analysts, might read the whole report and what are companies trying to achieve?

NED checklist

- Who is the reporting aimed at?
- Dependent on the size of company, have all CA2006 requirements been met?

- How does the company intend to use the reporting; is it more than just compliance?
- Has the right tone been set?
- Does the report illustrate appropriately the culture of the company?
- Has the business model – how the company makes money, adds and sustains value – been made clear?

Procedure

- As a NED it is important to understand the procedure for the writing and production of the narrative report the annual report and accounts.
  - Who is the author or authors?
  - Is it an end-of-year panic to complete or does it form a natural part of the company cycle and board calendar?
- Is the board given sufficient time to read, absorb, challenge and, if required, change, the narrative report? Remember that the contents of the annual report are issued in the name of all the directors.

Requirements

- Directors of all but micro companies are required to include a directors' report with the annual accounts filed at Companies House – details are included separately in these checklists.
- Directors of all but small and micro companies are required to include a strategic report with the annual accounts filed at Companies House. Details are included separately in the relevant checklists.
  - While the underlying expectation is 'true and fair', it is important from the independent stance of a NED to further challenge:
    - alignment to strategy and cohesion of approach
    - transparency and contextualisation
    - consistency and accuracy.

Further information

- Checklists:
  - directors' report, page 119
  - strategic report, page 257
- Various guidance on narrative reporting. Available at: www.frc.org.uk
- The Chartered Governance Institute: guidance note, 'Good practice for annual reports'.

Nomination committee

Introduction

Provision 17 of the UK Corporate Governance Code states:

> The board should establish a nomination committee to lead the process for appointments, ensure plans are in place for orderly succession to both the board and senior management positions, and oversee the development of a diverse pipeline for succession. A majority of members of the committee should be independent non- executive directors. The chair of the board should not chair the committee when it is dealing with the appointment of their successor.

The nomination committee needs to understand:

- the human interaction that has enabled the evolution of an organisation to reach its current position;
- the dynamics that exist between those around the board table (chair, executive directors, and non-executive directors);
- the interdependence of the senior management team; and
- the culture and ethos which underpins the people structure within the organisation.

A nomination committee member needs to get away from the meeting room and talk to people in the organisation to more effectively assess culture and need.

The 'pipeline' of talent must exist at all levels, not just around the board table. The nomination committee should not interfere with the normal appointment and recruitment process within the organisation, but alongside its board appointment role, it should be leading the company in setting people's expectations to underpin and develop the organisational culture.

- The 2018 FRC Guidance on Board Effectiveness contains a range of useful advice with regard to the activity of nomination committees including:
  - the nomination committee is responsible for board recruitment and will conduct a continuous and proactive process of planning

and assessment, taking into account the company's strategic priorities and the main trends and factors affecting the long-term success and future viability of the company (para 86);

- non-executive directors should possess a range of critical skills of value to the board and relevant to the challenges and opportunities facing the company (para 87);
- diversity in the board room can have a positive effect on the quality of decision making by reducing the risk of group think. With input from shareholders, boards need to decide which aspects of diversity are important in the context of the business and its needs (para 88);
- developing a more diverse executive pipeline is vital to increasing levels of diversity amongst those in senior positions (para 89); and
- skills matrices that map the existing skillset against that required to execute strategy and meet future challenges can be an effective way of identifying skills gaps. These are a useful tool for role evaluation and succession planning (para 93).

NED checklist

- Does your organisation have a properly constituted nomination committee?
- Are the terms of reference for the nomination committee reviewed and updated on an annual basis?
- Does the nomination committee proactively search for an appropriate diversity of skills and attributes when looking to recruit new executive and or non-executive directors?
- As a NED, do you believe that the nomination committee is appropriately challenging in its approach to both board recruitment and senior management oversight?
- Has the nomination committee assessed the skill set that is required for the board and its committees?
- Is the structure of the board reassessed to allow for the evolution of the organisation and emerging trends within its marketplace and sector?
- Has the board undertaken a skills audit?
- Does the nomination committee play a leading role (alongside the chair of the board) in the annual board and director evaluation process?
- Does the nomination committee ensure that the chair of the company is not involved in the recruitment and succession of that role?

- Does the nomination committee have an ongoing oversight to ensure an appropriate pipeline balance exists within the senior management team of the organisation, and its succession plan?

Requirements

- Provision 23 of the UK Corporate Governance Code requires that: the annual report should describe the work of the nomination committee, including:
  - the process used in relation to appointments, its approach to succession planning and how both support developing a diverse pipeline;
  - how the board evaluation has been conducted, the nature and extent of an external evaluator's contact with the board and individual directors, the outcomes of actions taken, and how it has or will influence board composition;
  - the policy on diversity and inclusion, its objectives and linkage to company strategy, how it has been implemented and progress on achieving the objectives; and
  - the gender balance of those in the senior management and their direct reports

Further information

- FRC: UK Corporate Governance Code (2018).
- FRC: Guidance on Board Effectiveness (2018).
- ICSA Publishing The Board Committees Handbook, chapter 9, Nomination Committee (2020).

Notice of meetings

Introduction

Receiving appropriate and timely notice of meetings, together with all required pre-meeting reading material, is essential for delivering effectiveness from any board or committee.

The required notice period for meetings will be dictated by:

- the constitution of the company;
- the law, for certain meetings; and
- company convention and accepted practice – although this may have developed through habit and not be delivering the most effective results.

The requirement and expectations for pre-meeting paperwork is left to the discretion, habit and discipline of each organisation and each group of people. It is right to suggest that the chair of the meeting should always establish and maintain the discipline around such matters but, in reality, this is not always the case.

Notice of meetings will usually be issued to participants by the company secretary or another administrator within an organisation. It is important that directors and other meeting participants know all relevant contact details for the 'administrator' of each meeting.

NED checklist

- Is the time, place and nature of every meeting always clear?
- Is the notice of meeting always received in an appropriate manner, and within the required timeframe?
- Are all relevant papers received ahead of meetings together with the notice of meeting, or if papers are to be accessed electronically is their repository clear? Is this far enough ahead of the meeting to enable constructive consideration?
- Do you know who to contact if you are unclear or uncertain about any aspect of a forthcoming meeting?

Procedure

- Model articles suggest:
  - any director may call a directors' meeting by giving notice of the meeting to the directors or by authorising the company secretary (if any) to give such notice; and
  - notice of a directors' meeting must be given to each director but need not be in writing.
- The Companies Act 2006 requires:
  - 21 days' notice for the AGM of a public company;
  - 14 days' notice for any other general meeting of a public company, or any general meeting of a private company; and
  - a member wishing to put a resolution to an AGM or EGM must give the company 28 days' notice.

Requirements

- A notice of meeting should contain:
  - company name;
  - date and time of meeting;
  - place of meeting;
  - details of dial-in or other web-based arrangements for electronic attendance;
  - nature of the business to be transacted (if the meeting is an AGM or an EGM for members of a company, then the notice must state this); and
  - details of accompanying or impending paperwork or documents for consideration ahead of the meeting.

Notes

- In today's electronic, connected world, it is easier for a notice of meeting, together with relevant accompanying documents to be either sent or accessible using the web. It is also easy for details to be changed ahead of meetings. It is important, therefore, for the administrator of a meeting to ensure that all meeting participants are clearly in receipt of the latest details and information with regard to any particular meeting.
- The constitution of a company should define whether the word 'days' means 'working days' or just 'general days'.
- The FRC Guidance on Board Effectiveness, paragraph 36, recommends that: 'To ensure there is sufficient time to consider the

issues, the notice of the AGM and related papers should be sent at least 20 working days before the AGM.'

Further information

- Companies House: model articles
- FRC: UK Corporate Governance Code (2018)
- FRC: Guidance on Board Effectiveness (2018).

People with significant control

Introduction

The People with Significant Control (PSC) Regulations 2016 apply to UK incorporated companies limited by shares and companies limited by guarantee (including community interest companies).

The PSC requirement is not applicable to UK companies that are subject to chapter 5 of the FCA's disclosure and transparency rules, where equivalent transparency is already available. This includes all companies with shares that are admitted to trading on a regulated market in the UK or the European economic area, or traded on specific markets in Switzerland, USA, Japan and Israel.

The transparency objective of the legislation is, at least in part, to help to combat tax evasion, money laundering and terrorist financing by providing a full picture of both the legal and the beneficial ownership of all businesses and organisations that are covered by the regulations. In effect, the PSC register is a register of natural persons involved in limited companies.

In recent years, the ability to search for information on a company that is registered at Companies House has been improved significantly, with an increasing ability to data search on a range of differing criteria. There has been a long-held desire by Companies House, BEIS and others for a similar searchable database of directors, and others who own and control legally constituted businesses.

Failure by a company (and therefore its directors and officers) to comply is a criminal offence punishable by imprisonment and or a fine. PSCs and other registrable relevant legal entities which fail to supply or update information or people who fail to comply with notices from a company relating to a PSC register might also have committed a criminal offence.

Any individual who believes that they are a PSC must ensure that their correct details are recorded for any organisation where they meet the required conditions.

NED checklist

- Have you reviewed the PSC register and its control implications for the company where you are a NED?
- Do you consider yourself to be a PSC? If so, are your details recorded correctly on the register?
- Does your company keep its own PSC register or just maintain the public record at Companies House?
- Ensuring that accurate PSC information is held correctly is part of your NED accountability.

Meaning of PSC

- There are five core conditions which determine whether a person is deemed to have significant influence or control within an organisation:
  - a person directly or indirectly holds more than 25% of the shares of the organisation;
  - a person directly or indirectly holds more than 25% of the voting rights of the organisation, where these are separate from or in addition to a shareholding within the organisation;
  - a person directly or indirectly holds the right to appoint or remove the majority of the directors of the organisation;
  - a person otherwise has the right to exercise, or actually exercises, significant influence or control within the organisation; and
  - where a trust or firm would satisfy one or more of the first four conditions, if it were an individual. Any individual who holds the right to exercise, or actually exercises, significant influence or control over the activities of that trust or firm.
- Significant influence or control is considered to exist if:
  - a person can direct the activities of a company, trust or firm, this would be indicative of 'control' of that organisation; and
  - a person can ensure that a company trust or firm generally adopts the activities which they desire, this would be indicative of that person holding "significant influence" over the operations of that organisation.
- Where an organisation is wholly or partly owned or significantly controlled by another legal entity rather than by one or more people, then that Relevant Legal Entity (RLE) must be recorded in the PSC register.
- The PSC register can never be empty. There are a number of permitted statements for circumstances where beneficial ownership is not established or unclear. In such situations one or more of such statements must be entered in the PSC register.

Information required on each PSC

- The information required for each PSC is:
  - Name.
  - Date of birth.
  - Nationality.
  - Country, state or part of the UK where the PSC usually lives.
  - Service address.
  - Usual residential address; unless this is the same as the service address.
  - The date when the individual became a PSC in relation to the company; for all companies in existence as at 6 April 2016, this date will be recorded as 6 April 2016; all movements thereafter will be recorded at the date where the person becomes or ceases to be a PSC.
  - Which of the five conditions for being a PSC the individual meets, with quantification of the level of interest where relevant.
  - Any restrictions on disclosing that a PSC's information is in place, such as a data protection order.
- The information required for an RLE is the organisational equivalent of the above personal information, including the registration number for any limited company who is an RLE.

Requirements

- All organisations that are covered by the PSC regulations must keep a register of individuals and legal entities that have control over them. This register must be kept with the statutory books and registers of the company and is a part of the incorporation process for new companies. Alternatively, a company can elect to keep its PSC register at Companies House, meaning that all information contained therein is on the public record.
- If a company chooses to maintain its own PSC register, then the information held by a company on its PSC register is required to be submitted and maintained on the central public register being held at Companies House; this has become part of the annual confirmation statement required from all limited companies.

Performance metrics

Introduction

The phrase 'performance metrics' is used to refer to any form of measure that a company might use and/or disclose, including not just financial metrics but also wider non-financial metrics which might be required under other international standards or frameworks.

The core objective of a performance metric has two dimensions:

- to recognise and illustrate change within an organisation; and
- to measure or correlate one measure of performance or activity within the organisation against a different aspect.

These measures might include but are not restricted to the key performance indicators (KPIs) that are a required part of reporting under CA2006.

The perpetual demand from regulators and analysts are that performance metrics are used to illustrate material and relevant aspects of business performance, and that the metrics are aligned to each other, to the wider financial and narrative reporting of an organisation, and where relevant and possible to the remuneration being received by the directors of the company.

NED checklist

- What are the performance metrics used by the board of directors to sense-check performance within the organisation?
- How appropriate, material and relevant are these performance metrics?
- As a NED, do you understand what is really being measured, and the integrity of the underlying data?
- When did the board last review the range and scope of the performance measures?
- Is there robust debate around the performance metrics at a board meeting or have they just become part of the habitual reporting pattern?

- Do the performance metrics help to identify the gaps?
- Do the performance metrics used by the directors align with the financial and narrative reporting, the published KPIs, and the financial results of the organisation?

Requirements

- A report from the FRC Financial Reporting Lab, entitled 'Performance Metrics – Principles and Practice', provides useful challenge and guidance in the production, analysis and consideration of such measures.
- The report suggests that performance metrics can and should derive from different types of operational dimension:
  - financial metrics directly aligned to GAAP reporting (e.g. operating profit);
  - financial metrics derived from but adjusted against GAAP reporting (e.g. earnings before interest, taxes, depreciation and amortisation (EBITDA);
  - non-monetary metrics based on standard measures (e.g. carbon emissions); and
  - non-monetary metrics with particular organisational relevance (e.g. customer satisfaction).
- The report suggests that there are five principles to deliver effective performance metrics:
  - Aligned to strategy: are the measures aligned to the organisational strategy and value drivers?
  - Transparent: why do we use these figures and where have they come from?
  - In context: what was expected, what has been achieved, and what is expected moving forwards?
  - Reliable: how are the measures developed and monitored?
  - Consistent: is the presentation and calculation similar or the same each year? Is there a track record of performance?

Further information

- FRC Financial Reporting Lab: report, 'Performance metrics' Available at: www.frc.org.uk/getattachment/cd978ef7-72ad-4785-81ee-e08bb7b7f152/LAB-Performance-metrics-FINAL.pdf.

Private or public company

Introduction

The majority of companies are private companies limited by shares (denoted by Ltd or Limited). Any exchange, transfer or selling of shares is usually within a defined and/or restricted membership and determined by the articles of association or an additional shareholder agreement.

The shares of a public company (denoted by PLC (public limited company)) in whole or in part can be open to investment by the public through a recognised stock exchange. This can be a useful means for such a company to raise capital; such companies are required to comply with significantly higher levels of regulation and governance expectation, together with enhanced reporting and transparency requirements.

A company designated as PLC does not have to trade its shares openly on a market, and may continue to be privately owned, with share movement restricted in accordance with its constitution. Any private limited company can apply to become a public limited company through application to Companies House and on proving that:

- it has at least £50,000 of issued share capital, with at least 25% having been paid up (funds received from shareholders);
- it has two directors;
- it has a company secretary meeting the professional requirements of CA2006; and
- it files full accounts.

NED checklist

- While the LTD or PLC status of the company where you are a NED should be clear to you at the outset, are you certain of the status of key competitors, customers and suppliers?
- If you are a NED in a private limited company, ensure you have a good working knowledge of the constitution of your company, and the requirements of directors under CA2006, together with any related expectations based upon the size of your company:

- ▷ Do you meet the size criteria which require you to apply the Wates Principles on corporate governance?
- ▷ Do you meet the size criteria which require enhanced CA2006 s.172 reporting?

- If you are a NED in a public limited company, ensure you have a good working knowledge of the same requirements as a private limited company, but in addition the governance and market expectations that apply to your company, and to you as a director of a PLC.

Notes

- The denoting of Ltd or Limited might also refer to a company limited by guarantee, where generally each member holds one share, and acts as an equal guarantor under the constitution rather than a shareholder.

Further information

- Companies House: reference material.
- ICSA Publishing: The Non-Executive Directors' Handbook (2019)

Professional advice and guidance

Introduction

While many aspects of being a director, and the associated duties of a director, are obvious, straightforward and based upon common sense, other aspects of the law and expectations of a director are complex and require a deeper level of understanding than is necessary on a normal day-to-day basis.

It is important for a director to know where to turn for professional advice and guidance.

Principle 16 of the 2018 UK Corporate Governance Code states:

> All directors should have access to the advice of the company secretary, who is responsible for advising the board on all governance matters.

There may, however, be occasions where a director wishes to seek external professional advice to garner an objective opinion on a particular matter of importance. This potential requirement should be pre-empted by the company either in the terms of engagement of a director or within any internal directors' handbook or code of practice.

Additionally, the terms of reference for each board committee should enable the members of that committee to seek professional external advice with regard to their particular responsibilities without the need to first seek board approval.

Unless the advice that is required is of an entirely personal nature with regard to the relationship between an individual director and the company or the company's activities, it is reasonable to expect that the company will fund any such external advice that is required for a director to fulfil their role professionally, correctly and within the law.

NED checklist

- Is there a clear policy on how and when external professional advice can be requested either individually by a director or collectively?
- Where is this reflected – service contract, committee terms of reference? What is the procedure? Can directors seek independent

professional advice or do they need to use company advisers? When was this policy last updated?

- If there is a maximum amount of expenditure included in such a policy, is the amount still appropriate?

Quorum requirements

Introduction

The quorum for a meeting is the minimum number of appropriately approved people who must be present and entitled to vote in order to constitute a valid meeting.

At a general meeting of shareholders, the quorum will be the minimum number of members that are required to vote on any resolution, in accordance with the constitution of the company. In the absence of any particular provision in the articles of association (articles) the default quorum is two members (unless, of course, a company only has one member). The articles of a company may further stipulate that a required percentage of shares in issue are represented at a meeting to enable it to be quorate.

At a meeting of the directors of a company, the quorum will be the minimum number of directors that are required to be present (in person or participating electronically) and are entitled to vote at such a meeting. The articles will normally stipulate the quorum, the presumption within the model articles for both private and public companies is two directors (unless a company only has one director). They will usually enable directors to amend the required quorum for future meetings but any such change must be approved at a meeting where the quorum meets the current requirement.

NED checklist

- Ensure that the required quorum for a meeting of directors or shareholders, is clear from the articles.
- At the start of each meeting ensure that the meeting is quorate.
- Ensure that all decisions and key discussions take place while the meeting continues to maintain a quorum. This is of particular importance if a decision is required involving one or more directors who are excluded from voting due to a conflict of interests.

Reduction of capital

Introduction

Companies may reduce capital by buying back their own shares for a number of reasons, including: a lack of viable investment opportunities, to create shareholder value by reducing the number of shares in issue which increases earnings per share and to make a distribution of cash more tax-efficient for shareholders compared to the payment of a cash dividend.

The Companies Act 2006 enables a company to reduce its share capital through a number of alternative methods. It is important that the correct procedures are followed, dependent upon the type of company and any restrictions within its constitution.

The purpose of any proposed reduction of capital should be discussed and agreed by all directors.

It is advisable for directors to seek the advice of one or more appropriate experienced professionals (e.g. accountant, lawyer, company secretary).

- Public and private companies can reduce their share capital by special resolution of the members and subject to confirmation by the court.
- A private company may reduce its share capital by special resolution of the members, provided the resolution is supported by a solvency statement.
- A private company may alternatively reduce its share capital but proposing to make small value purchases of shares.

A public company may only reduce its share capital by court order. The role of the court is to ensure that the interests of creditors and shareholders are protected.

NED checklist

- Check the articles of association to ensure there is no restriction on reduction of capital.

- If the company is a PLC, will the reduction result in the issued share capital falling below the minimum share capital requirement?
- If the intention in a private company is to make small value purchases of shares to reduce the share capital, then the articles of association must contain authority for the company to purchase its own shares.
- At least one issued share must remain in a company following the completion of any reduction of capital.
- Will all directors sign any required declaration of solvency?

Procedure

- If the proposed reduction of capital requires a court order, the application to the court must be made through a special resolution from within a general meeting of the company. This will have been preceded by a proposal to the shareholders from the directors of the company. If the court approved the special resolution all relevant documents must be submitted to Companies House within the required timeframe.
- If the proposed reduction of capital in a private company is to be through a special resolution of the members supported by a solvency statement, a directors' meeting must approve the giving of the solvency statement, recommending the reduction of capital to members. This recommendation must be approved either through a general meeting or through the circulation of a written resolution requiring members' approval. Upon approval, all relevant documents must be submitted to Companies House within the required timeframe.
- If the proposed reduction of capital in a private company is to be through the simplified process of small value purchase of its own shares, the proposed contract of purchase must be made available for inspection by members of the company not less than 15 days prior to the general meeting at which the resolution is to be considered.

Notes

- A private company may authorise the purchase of its own shares by written resolution under s, 288 of CA2006. To be valid, a copy of the proposed contract or a memorandum of its terms must be made available to each member no later than the date on which the written resolution is forwarded to them for approval and signature. In practice, it is normal to circulate a copy of the contract or the memorandum, together with a written resolution for signature and return.

Register of directors

Introduction

All companies are required to maintain a register of directors which must be kept and available for inspection at the registered office or the Single Alternative Inspection Location (SAIL) (see page 253). The information held for each director who is a natural person must include:

- Current and any former names (within the past 20 years)
- Service address
- Nationality
- Business occupation
- Date of birth.

Directors have two addresses registered against their names at Companies House:

- Service address: this is the registered office of the company and (by default and/or selection) will be used for all official notices.
- Usual residential address: this is not visible on the public register unless accepted as such by a director.

A company must keep a separate register of directors' residential addresses.

The shareholders/directors of a private company may elect to keep their register of directors on the central register. If such an election includes the register of usual residential addresses it is worth noting that this removes the confidentiality purpose of such a register, with all details being available on the public record at Companies House.

NED checklist

- Are the address and other details held by the company correct?
- Is the register of residential addresses held at the registered office, and hence residential address details are not on the public record?

- Is there a clear policy (operating within legal requirements) with regard to the maintenance, holding and inspection (if requested) of registers?

Further information

- Companies House.

Registered office

Introduction

All companies must have an address at which legal documents can be served. This is known as the registered office.

The first registered office of a company will be the address detailed on the incorporation form IN01.

Any change in registered office must be notified to Companies House on form AD01 to be effective. The registered office must be situated in the country of registration.

The registered office address must be shown on the company's business stationery, emails and its website(s).

Statutory records of the company are usually retained at the registered office. However, an alternative address may be selected where statutory records may be kept and inspected. This is known as the Single Alternative Inspection Location (SAIL). Companies must advise Companies House of the use of a SAIL.

Although most of the administrative and procedural matters will be handled by the company secretary, accountability lies equally with all officers of the company. if there is no company secretary, then the directors (jointly and several) are accountable for ensuring that due procedure is followed.

NED checklist

- Is the proposed registered office address in the country of incorporation and is the address a physical building (PO box addresses are not permitted)?
- Is the company's name displayed at the registered office?
- Does the registered office address appear correctly on these documents?
  - business letters, e-mails and other correspondence
  - other stationery

  - invoices and order forms
  - brochures and other marketing material
  - website(s).
- Is there a SAIL location or are the statutory registers kept, and available for inspection at the registered office?
- If the registered office is changed, have the statutory registers been moved to the new location?

Procedure

- Convene a directors' meeting to approve a change in registered office address, which must be approved at a valid and quorate meeting of directors.
- Any change in address must be submitted to Companies House on form AD01 and notified to bankers, auditors, solicitors, HMRC and other interested persons.
- All relevant documents must show any changed registered office address no later than 14 days after the date that the notice of change was submitted to Companies House.

Further information

- Companies House.

Related party transactions

Introduction

A related party transaction exists where a director, or a person 'connected' with a director, acquires a material non-cash asset from the company or disposes of such an asset to the company.

In most instances such a transaction should be approved by the shareholders of the company.

A material transaction is a matter of judgement and depends on the amount and on the entity involved. Many companies may have a rule of thumb assuming, for example, that if the value of a transaction falls under a 5% threshold it is not material.

If the director or the connected person is also a director of the company's holding company, then approval of the members of the holding company must also be sought.

NED checklist

- Have any related party transactions taken place during the year?
- Who is responsible for the notification of related party transactions?
- Have they been discussed and minuted correctly at a directors' meeting?
- Has approval been obtained from members in accordance with the law and/or the constitution of the company?
- Has any required note been included in the annual report and accounts of the company?

Procedure

- A directors' meeting should recommend an appropriate special resolution to members and thus convene a general meeting to seek approval by written resolution in the case of a private company.

Notes

- Transactions between companies of a wholly owned group do not require approval.
- Where a transaction has not received approval of the members, the transaction will usually be voidable by the company.
- Where a transaction was not approved in advance, it may be affirmed by members within a reasonable period.
- Where a director acquires a non-cash asset by virtue of being a member of the company, approval is not required.
- Any arrangements entered into which have not received prior or retrospective approval between a director, connected person or holding company and the company make that director or connected person liable to the company for any gain arising out of the transaction or any losses suffered by the company.

Further information

- ICSA Publishing: The Non-Executive Directors' Handbook (2019).

Remuneration committee

Introduction

Provision 32 of the UK Corporate Governance Code states:

> The board should establish a remuneration committee of independent non-executive directors, with a minimum membership of three, or in the case of smaller companies, two. In addition, the chair of the board can only be a member if they were independent on appointment and cannot chair the committee. Before appointment as chair of the remuneration committee, the appointee should have served on a remuneration committee for at least twelve months.

The remuneration of executive directors and other senior executives is an important and emotive aspect of corporate governance and an increasing focus for shareholder activism in listed companies. It is important that the board and the remuneration committee devote an appropriate amount of time to ensuring that the remuneration policy is fair, aligned and robust.

It is important for the board of directors, through effective use of the remuneration committee, to attempt to achieve an optimal balance. Remuneration needs to be sufficiently attractive to persuade talented individuals to work for the company while not risking the reputation of the company through seeming to be over-rewarding the executive directors and senior managers.

Paragraph 129 of the FRC Guidance on Board Effectiveness states:

> The remuneration committee has delegated responsibility for designing and determining remuneration for the chair, executive directors and the next level of senior management. It is vital that the remuneration committee recognises and manages potential conflicts of interest in this process.

Paragraph 130 advises:

> The remuneration committee is also tasked with reviewing workforce remuneration and related policies. The purpose of this review is to:
>
> - ensure the reward, incentives and conditions available to the company's workforce are taken into account when deciding the pay of executive directors and senior management;

- enable the remuneration committee to explain to the workforce each year how decisions on executive pay reflect wider company pay policy; and
- enable the remuneration committee to feedback to the board on workforce reward, incentives and conditions, and support the latter's monitoring of whether company policies and practices support culture and strategy.

Paragraph 133 advises:

> The design of remuneration policies, structures and schemes is a crucial part of the remuneration committee's role. Remuneration committees are expected to focus on the strategic rationale for executive pay and the links between remuneration, strategy and long-term sustainable success.

Paragraph 136 advises

> Remuneration committees are encouraged to be innovative and work with shareholders to simplify the structure of the remuneration policy.

Given the heightened levels of media, shareholder and societal interest in levels of director remuneration and perceptions of inequality, it is important that NEDs in particular ensure a robust and professional approach to all matters of remuneration within an organisation.
To undertake this effectively and appropriately requires far more understanding and detail than can be provided in a simplified checklist entry.

NED checklist

- Is the remuneration committee correctly structured and are its terms of reference reviewed on an annual basis?
- Do the NEDs play a leading role in bringing objectivity and experience to the board of directors as a whole in its wider consideration of executive director and senior management remuneration?
- How is executive director remuneration aligned with wider company pay policy?
- Has executive director remuneration been appropriately linked to the strategy of the company, the outcome of strategic objectives, performance metrics and other KPIs?
- Does the company have an appropriate policy in place to explain to the workforce how executive pay arrangements are aligned with wider company pay policy?
- Does the remuneration committee understand the total amount that is potentially being awarded to each executive director, and what circumstances will enable that reward and the rationale behind it?

- Has the board of directors as a whole considered placing a monetary limit on the level of remuneration available to executive directors and senior managers?

Procedure

- Remuneration of non-executive directors should be determined in accordance with the constitution or by the board as a whole. Levels of remuneration should reflect the time commitment and responsibilities of the role. Remuneration for all non-executive directors should not include share options or other performance related elements.

Requirements

- Provision 41 of the UK Corporate Governance Code states:

  There should be a description of the work of the remuneration committee in the annual report, including:

  - an explanation of the strategic rationale for executive directors' remuneration policies, structures and any performance metrics;
  - reasons why the remuneration is appropriate using internal and external measures, including pay ratios and pay gaps;
  - a description, with examples, of how the remuneration committee has addressed aspects of clarity, simplicity, risk, predictability, proportionality, and cultural alignment in the remuneration packages being paid to directors and senior managers;
  - whether the remuneration policy operated as intended in terms of company performance and quantum, and, if not, what changes are necessary;
  - what engagement has taken place with shareholders and the impact this has had on remuneration policy and outcomes;
  - what engagement with the workforce has taken place to explain how executive remuneration aligns with wider company pay policy; and
  - to what extent discretion has been applied to remuneration outcomes and the reasons why.

Notes

The Companies Act 2006 requires quoted companies to prepare a directors' remuneration report, which must be approved by the board. This can be included in the report on the work of the remuneration committee (above) and is usually issued as part of the annual report and accounts. The Companies Act 2006 now provides that the remuneration report should contain:

- a statement by the chair of the remuneration committee;
- a statement of the company's policy on directors' remuneration which sets out how the company proposes to pay its directors; and
- an implementation report, containing details of the remuneration of each director and information about how remuneration policy was implemented during the financial year.

Shareholders should have a binding vote on an ordinary resolution to approve the remuneration policy, every three years and an annual vote on the implementation report, which is advisory only.

Further information

- FRC: UK Corporate Governance Code (2018).
- FRC: Guidance on Board Effectiveness (2018).
- Companies Act 2006.
- ICSA Publishing: The Non-Executive Directors' Handbook, chapter 7, Remuneration committee (2019).

Rights issue

Introduction

A rights issue is an issue of shares to any existing shareholder pro rata to their existing holdings. A shareholder in a company is entitled, by right of their shareholding, to maintain the percentage ownership of that company if the number of shares in issue is increased. Hence they are entitled to a proportionate percentage of any new issue of shares by right. Shareholders can also vote to set aside their rights (e.g. in the event of an acquisition for shares).

Rights issues are used by companies to obtain additional funding from the company's shareholders rather than obtaining working capital by borrowing from banks or other financial institutions.

Any such new issue of shares will be proposed by the directors of the company in accordance with the constitution of the company,

NED checklist

- Check the articles of association of the company and make certain you are aware of the authority and ability of directors to authorise new share issues within the company.
- Be certain of any restrictions or maximum number of shares that may be issued.

Procedure

- A formally constituted meeting of directors will be required to approve a resolution declaring a rights issue of shares. It is important that such a meeting is quorate.
- As part of the NED oversight and challenge role, it is important to be satisfied that all appropriate procedures with regard to a rights issue, including the communication with the company's shareholders, are appropriate and represent the best interests and reputation of the company.

Risk appetite and tolerance

Introduction

Risk appetite refers to the 'hunger' for risk of an individual or an organisation. It exists on the dynamic that runs between risk aversion and risk seeking. Approach to risk is always based upon an individual 'appetite', around a board table, or within an organisation. The 'appetite' can be identified as the cumulative 'appetites' of the drivers of the strategy and strategic direction of the company.

Risk tolerance is required in the real world by both risk averters and risk seekers. Acceptable levels of tolerance are measured from the interaction of relative impact and likelihood on the organisation or the strategic objectives. In most organisations (or people) there will be natural clusters of acceptability. Thus 'risk tolerance' will often be based upon the judgements of the people involved. These judgements are being made by the same people who potentially wish for something to happen or not happen, therefore their judgement may well be skewed in favour of, or against, a particular opportunity or risk.

NED checklist

- Is the organisational risk appetite defined, understood by directors and aligned appropriately to the strategy of the organisation?
- Are the risk tolerance levels defined, understood by directors and aligned appropriately to the ongoing operational activities of the organisation?
- If risk appetite and/or risk tolerance has not appeared on your board agenda within the last six months, then ensure it appears on the next agenda.

Requirements

- Principle O of the UK Corporate Governance Code states:

  The board should establish procedures to manage risk, oversee the internal control framework, and determine the nature and extent of the principal risks the company is willing to take in order to achieve its long-term strategic objectives.

- The directors as a whole and the audit committee in particular (comprised of independent NEDs) must have a clear understanding of the organisational risk appetite, and the inevitable difference in risk appetites of directors, senior managers and influences within the organisation.

Notes

- A *risk-averse* person (or group (of people)) looks for certainty of outcome and is therefore prepared to sacrifice opportunities that might exist for change. Risk aversion can often lead to an intolerance of challenge and therefore an overreaction to any threat to the status quo. Facts are often preferred to theories.
- A *risk-seeking* person (or group (of people)) accepts that life is full of options and uncertainty and such a person has confidence in using their abilities to counter whatever they may face. Threats that are seen by the risk-averse person are very often not even considered as threats by the risk-seeking person. Risk seeking can often lead to a dangerous dismissal of the realities that confront a person or organisation.

Further information

- FRC: Guidance on Risk Management, Internal Control and Related Financial and Business Reporting (2014).
- ICSA Publishing: The Non-Executive Directors' Handbook, chapter 10, Internal Control and Risk Management (2019).
- Wates Principles on Corporate Governance (2018).

Risk – the three lines of defence

Introduction

Many organisations have adopted and implemented (or at least claim to) a modular approach to control of risk, referred to as the *'three lines of defence'* ('Three lines'). The starting point for this is the model itself, which illustrates the separation between

- the operational ownership and management of risk within the organisation;
- the professional oversight of risk within the organisation; and
- the objective consideration of risk from an independent, if sometimes internal, perspective.

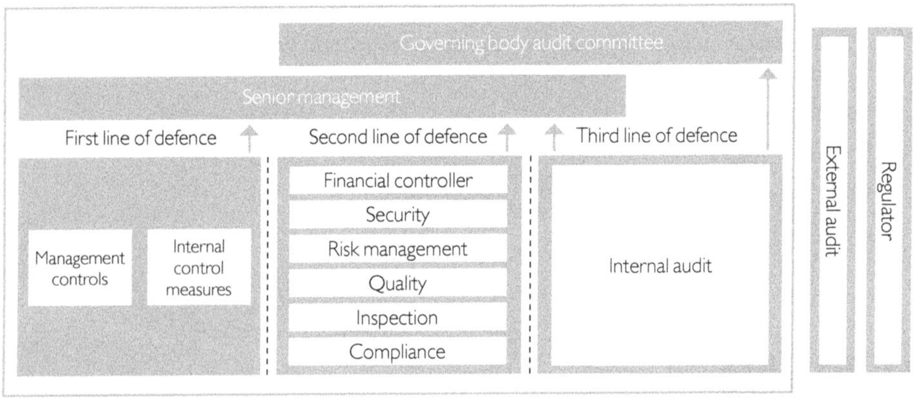

NED checklist

- Does your organisation use a 'three lines' approach to risk? If not, what approach does your organisation take and who is in control of the process?
- Are the directors clear on the role they are expected to fulfil within the second and third lines?

- Is there a clarity of risk management and control within the organisation?
- Is the organisational control structure fit for purpose?

Procedure within the 'three lines' structure

- The first line of defence includes control measures that have been built into the internal processes and the direct management oversight and control of risk within the organisation. These controls are accountable to the senior management, who in turn are accountable to those empowered with governance, often through a direct interaction with the audit committee comprising of Independent NEDs.
- The second line of defence includes a range of professional control functions, each empowered with the scrutiny, oversight and control off the direct risks of the organisation. These people are likewise accountable to the senior management, who in turn are accountable to those empowered with governance, these professionals will frequently have a direct interaction and reporting line (straight or dotted) to the audit committee comprising of independent NEDs.
- The third line of defence is the internal audit function within an organisation. This is depicted as having a dual reporting structure, to both senior management and those empowered with governance. The link between the internal audit function and the audit committee is often perceived as a firm reporting line.

Requirements

- The UK Corporate Governance Code and the related guidance suggests that where an internal audit function does not exist, an important role for the NEDs on the audit committee is to assess, on at least an annual basis, this perceived gap in the control structure.

Notes

- As with many such modular approaches, it has become common for organisations to claim that the use of the 'three lines' is their approach to the control of the risks that are aligned with their strategy.
- They will report on this accordingly in an attempt to illustrate their control effectiveness.
- The variability and depth of reporting in this area suggests a dichotomy exists between those who report and actually practice the 'three lines' principles, and of those who simply use it as an indication of potential control.

Risk committee

Introduction

The board of directors as a whole has accountability for risk. It is important that 'risk' is a regular item for all directors to debate, challenge and understand.

Principle O of the UK Corporate Governance Code (UK Code) states:

> The board should establish procedures to manage risk, oversee the internal control framework,and determine the nature and extent of the principal risks the company is willing to take in order to achieve its long-term strategic objectives.'

In many organisations the initial consideration of risk and control is delegated to the audit committee: sometimes, this committee is retitled as the audit and risk committee. This is supported by Provision 25 of the UK Code which suggests that one of the main roles and responsibilities of the audit committee is:

> 'reviewing the company's internal financial controls and internal control and risk management systems, unless expressly addressed by a separate board risk committee composed of independent NEDs, or by the board itself'.

A board may establish a risk committee, as an additional committee of the board.

What remains important is that there is a robust and regular consideration and challenge of all matters pertaining to risk within the company. That there is a clarity of where the risk debate will take place. That the board of directors, as a whole, receive regular and transparent risk reports as they will always retain the ultimate accountability to the shareholders and stakeholders.

NED checklist

- Where is the primary debating and challenge point for risk in the company?
- Who has oversight of risk, the board as a whole or another committee?

- If there is no formal risk committee, is this incorporated into the role of audit committee and reflected in the audit committee terms of reference?
- If there is a formal risk committee does it have appropriate terms of reference and clear lines of accountability?
- Does the organisation maintain a 'live' and relevant risk register? How is this aligned to the reporting of risk to directors? Does the raw data and its later interpretation have integrity within the organisation?
- Whatever the solution, are you as a NED satisfied that all appropriate debate and challenge is applied to the risks faced by the company that you, jointly with the other directors, are responsible for leading?

Procedure

- The board of directors must decide where risk is to be debated and challenged in the first instance before being reported to the board as a whole.
- If the board decide on a risk committee, then it should be correctly constituted, should report regularly to the board as a whole, and a report of its activities should be included in the annual report and accounts.
- If the board decides that the audit committee is to be the primary debating point for risk the terms of reference of the audit committee should be amended to reflect this. The audit committee should report on risk to the board on a regular basis and include a section on risk in the audit committee report in the annual report and accounts.
- If the board decide to retain primary debate on risk for themselves as a board, this should be reflected in the minutes of the company and also in the annual report and accounts.

Requirements

- The core areas for consideration by the risk committee, the audit committee and/or the board as a whole should include:
  - risk appetite and tolerance in alignment with the strategy of the company;
  - short and longer-term perspectives of risk and viability;
  - risk assessment and transparency of risk reporting within the organisation;
  - risk assessment before material decisions are made;
  - appropriate policies with regard to risk; employees should receive regular training; and

- how the directors and senior management respond to matters of risk.

Further information

- The Chartered Governance Institute: guidance note, 'Terms of reference for the risk committee'.
- ICSA Publishing: The Non-Executives Directors' Handbook, chapter 10, Internal control and risk management (2019).

Risk register

Introduction

The variety and complexity of the risks faced by most organisations inevitably leads to the construction of a formal framework to allow the organisation to list, categorise, and give a relevance and rating to the multiplicity of risks that face them.

It is common for this structure to be referred to as the risk register of the organisation, although such structures appear in many different shapes and sizes.

The size and complexity of a risk register usually derives from:

- the hierarchical level of management driving the initiative;
- the interest level of the those entrusted with the compilation;
- the resources available; and
- the level of applied technology within the organisation.

NED checklist

- Does a risk register exist?
  - Is it a 'live' document or system that is constantly updated?
  - Is it used as an active tool in the business, or is it just a flat reporting document?
- As a NED, how often do you see the risk register(s)?
  - Are you assured that you are seeing the most relevant risks?
  - If you only see highlights in either a report or a diagram, do you know how many risks exist on the register?
- Does each risk have an owner who is genuinely accountable?
- How often is the risk register updated?
- Who decides on rating and prioritisation of risks, and how?

Procedure

- Creating a risk register should be part of the strategic decision making of an organisation. The suggested starting point should not be how to create the register, but what is the register to be used for?
- If the ultimate objective is a refined report of core risks for a monthly board meeting, then the approach will need to be different to an expectation of an all-encompassing database of every risk that the organisation has and does face.
- It is important that the organisation and the owner(s), (compiler(s) and updater(s)) of the register have a unified vision of what is required. Experience suggests that the managing director, the accountant, the operations manager, the health and safety manager, other managers, and the 'poor' employee entrusted with the task will have significantly different views of the structure, the layout and the intention of a risk register.
- To achieve success there needs to be a common understanding of the need, the expectation and the method and timeframe for delivery.

Requirements

- The following is a non-exclusive suggestion for some aspects that might be contained within a risk register. It is more important to include a smaller number of live, challenging and meaningful risks than to try to capture everything in an organisation that might pose a risk.
  - A description of the risk restricted to a few relevant words.
  - A means of rating each risk against other risks – impact, probability, tolerance levels etc.
  - Ownership of the risk – who is monitoring activity?
  - Dates of first entry and subsequent actions.
  - Risk mitigation activities.

Notes

- It is entirely up to each organisation to decide whether and how it maintains a risk register.
- What matters is that the risk register is a 'live' and 'living' structure that helps directors in the monitoring and control of risk.

Role clarity

Introduction

In every company there are several formal director and officer roles which need to be undertaken, some by statute and some by operational requirement.

The exact nature and expectations of each role is largely left to each individual company to define; this is true even where there is a statutory underpinning of the role, such as the duties of a director or the expectations of a company secretary.

It is important, therefore, to understand the parameters of each role, their areas of speciality, their areas of mutuality, and their areas of crossover. The parameters below are a guideline of expectation, but each company is likely have a slightly different interpretation of expectations and boundaries.

NED checklist

- Are you certain of the boundaries and expectation of your role as a NED?
- How does and must your NED role interact with the other roles within your company?
- Is there a clarity between the expectation of a NED, and the expectations and operational oversight of an executive director?
- Do you have a role matrix? If not, encourage someone to develop one as it can act as a useful 'gap' analysis tool for the governance oversight of a business.

Requirements

- Provision 14 of the UK Corporate Governance Code 2018 states:

  > The responsibilities of the chair, chief executive, senior independent director, board and committees should be clear, set out in writing, agreed by the board and made publicly available.

Role parameters

- Chair:
  - Leader of the board and responsible for its effectiveness.
  - Setting the board agenda – not just each meeting, but from a more holistic perspective.
  - Maintain the appropriate focus on strategy, performance, value-creation, culture, stakeholders and director accountability.
  - Evolve a board culture which sets the 'tone from the top' and oversees effective governance of the organisation.
  - Ensure all directors are involved in challenge and debate at the optimal level for their differing skill and experience, supporting the role of the senior independent director (SID).
  - Foster relationships between executive and non-executive directors, in particular establishing a robust and challenging working relationship between chair and CEO.
  - Oversee and ensure engagement of directors with induction, training, development, board and director evaluation.
- Chief executive officer (CEO) or managing director:
  - Leader of the business and responsible for the delivery of the strategic objectives established by the board.
  - An executive director of the business.
  - Operates under the powers delegated from the board, and within the remit and expectations of their contract.
  - Builds an effective relationship with the chair and other key directors.
  - Ensures that the required standards of governance are understood and applied throughout the business.
  - Keeps the board advised of views and trends that emerge within both the management team and the workforce.
  - Ensures delivery of appropriate and timely management and operational information to the board.
  - Manages and oversees the executive directors.
- Chief financial officer (CFO) or finance director:
  - Leads and oversees all aspects of the financial operation of the business, under the strategic objectives established by the board.
  - Usually directly accountable to the CEO but with a 'dotted line' to the board.
  - An executive director of the business.

- Builds, develops and leads a finance team to deliver assurance to the board and the shareholders.
- Constant awareness of the short-term (going concern) and longer-term viability of the business through astute liquidity oversight and management.
- Development and presentation of appropriate management accounting information for the board and the business, leading to oversight and initial ownership of the statutory financial reporting of the business.
- Encourages and develop the financial literacy within the board and senior management.

- Executive director:
  - Accountable for a focused operational aspect of the business and for delivery of the strategic objectives established by the board.
  - Usually directly accountable to the CEO.
  - An executive director of the business.
- Senior independent director (SID):
  - Appointed by the board from amongst the independent non-executive directors.
  - Provides a sounding board for the chair.
  - An intermediary, when required, between chair, directors and/or shareholders.
  - Leads evaluation of the chai's role and ensures appropriate succession planning when appropriate.
- Non-executive directors (NED):
  - No executive role within the business.
  - Membership and leadership of board committees as required.
  - Challenge and oversight of the effective governance and performance of the business on behalf of the shareholders.
  - Ideally 'independent' in so far as no other relationship with the business but may be (e.g.) a family director. Whatever the nature of the role, remember that s. 173 of CA2006 requires all directors to maintain and independence of attitude and approach.
  - Many other aspects as identified throughout this text.
- Company secretary:
  - Appointed by the directors, and for a public company in accordance with the requirements of CA2006.
  - Responsible for ensuring compliance with board procedures.
  - Advising board and directors on all governance matters.

- Supporting the chair and the NEDs, and helping the board and its committees to function efficiently.
- An officer of the company who stands *pari passu* with the directors concerning their many accountabilities and duties under the law.

Further information

- FRC: Guidance on Board Effectiveness (2018).
- ICSA Publishing: The Non-Executive Directors' Handbook, chapter 5 (2019).

Scepticism

Introduction

The dictionary definition of sceptical has two dimensions:

- a sceptical attitude; doubt as to the truth of something; and
- a more philosophical belief that certain knowledge is impossible.

The Greek origin of scepticism is the word 'skepsis' which translates as examination, inquiry into, and hesitation or doubt. The philosophical development of this idea has led to three concepts:

- Doubt stimulates informed challenge and inquiry.
- All judgement about truth must be suspended – we need to keep an open mind.
- Ideas are not finite – we are regularly forced to make decisions despite our continuing propensity to doubt.

A fundamental concept within the accounts of a company is that of 'true and fair'.

Section 393 of CA2006 states:

> The directors of a company must not approve the accounts...unless they are satisfied that they give a **true and fair** view of the assets, liabilities, financial position and profit or loss of the company or group.

Our numeracy structure, the principles of double entry accounting, and all other such formats, rely on us being able to provide a logical trail of figures from raw data to refined information. However, we are then required to reconsider such 'true' figures within the context of the organisation and its wider stakeholder environment, and thus ensure that the figures we are using as final information are being stated from a 'fair' position. This does not just apply at the very end of the process as we finalise the published year-end financial accounts, a plethora of different judgements by different people have been made at very differing levels within an organisation.

Judgement requires the use of the sceptical human brain to challenge and enquire, but then to still make a decision. The accounts that we sign as *true and fair,* in our name as directors of the company have been subject to the judgements and biases many decisions and many brains.

Scepticism is a core requirement from all directors, but especially from the objective independence of the NED.

NED checklist

- How sceptical are you as a NED? Remember that scepticism is different from cynicism – the latter is negative, the former is positive. A NED is required to bring a sceptical and challenging mind to all aspect of boardroom discussion and decision making. The NED has the luxury of not being involved in the day-to-day habits of the organisations, so is required to stand back and challenge objectively.
- When did you, as a NED, last ask a challenging question during a board meeting?
- Do you understand the finances and accounts of your business sufficiently to be able to bring the required scepticism to a set of accounts based upon 'true and fair' principles?
- Do you understand what is 'true' in your company's accounts and what is 'fair'?
- Do you understand the operational activities of the business sufficiently to bring appropriate sceptical challenge?
- Do you know the decision makers throughout the business sufficiently well to know where and when to bring appropriate sceptical challenge?
- Do you know yourself well enough to be able to recognise and stand aside from your own biases?

Notes

- An Association of Chartered Certified Accountants (ACCA) publication on professional scepticism suggests 12 biases that we ought to be sceptically aware of when considering the finances and position of a company:

Hindsight	Being wise after the event
Outcome	Results rather than origination
Confirmation	Selecting what agrees with our existing beliefs
Anchoring	Using a benchmark to judge
Availability	Only using what is in front of us
Groupthink	Fitting in with the crowd – 'when in Rome…'

Overconfidence	We know better
Recency	Not looking far enough back
Conjunction	Predefined linkage in our minds
Selectivity	Not looking beyond the obvious
Stereotyping	Box thinking
Blind-spot	Lack of 360^0 vision

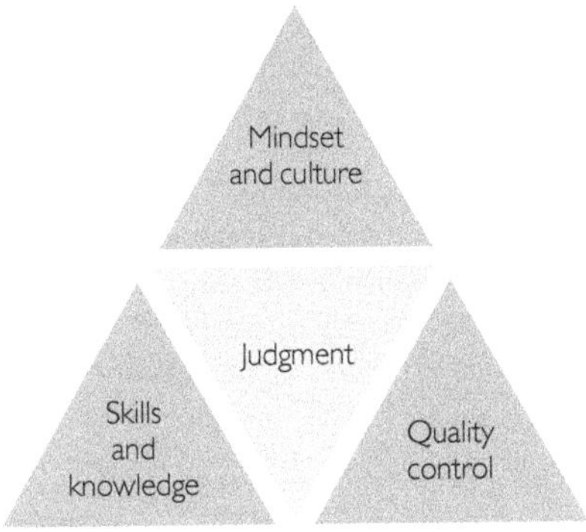

In 2015, the FRC issued a document entitled 'Audit Quality – Practice aid for audit committees' which contains useful and detailed recommendations for the audit committee in their support, encouragement and oversight of the external auditors and the external audit process. It is based around a recognition of the significance of 'judgment' throughout the audit process. The FRC model suggests this is underpinned by three aspects:

- Mindset and culture.
- Skills character and knowledge.
- Quality control.

Further information

- ACCA: 'Banishing Bias'. Available at: www.accaglobal.com/content/dam/ACCA_Global/Technical/audit/pi-banishing-bias-prof-scepticism.pdf.
- FRC: 'Audit Quality – Practice aid for audit committees'.

Senior independent director

Introduction

The role of senior independent director (SID) was first suggested by the Higgs Review in 2003 and became an expectation from listed companies in the Revised Code of Corporate Governance issued by the FRC later in 2003. It has become an accepted part of the 'comply or explain' provisions of all subsequent corporate governance codes. Provision 12 of the 2018 Code states:

> The Board should appoint one of the independent non-executive directors to be the senior independent director to provide a sounding board for the chair and serve as an intermediary for the other directors and shareholders.

NED checklist

- Who is the SID?
- Are the expectations from the SID role, as outlined below, met within the format and structure of the board meetings and annual board agenda?
- Is it clear when the SID should intervene to maintain board and company stability, and does this happen?

Procedure

- The SID should be appointed by the board of directors from amongst the independent NEDs of the company.
- The SID should always be available for confidential discussion with the chair, the chief executive, and any other director of the company.
- The SID should be available to shareholders of the company when they have concerns that cannot or have failed to be satisfied through the normal communication channels, or where the normal route is inappropriate.

Requirements

- In general terms the requirements from the SID are to:
  - work closely with the chair, providing support and acting as a sounding board;
  - act as an intermediary for other directors as and when required;
  - meet at least annually with the other NEDs without the chair or the EDs present. Part of the purpose of this meeting will be to review the performance of the chair, and when required, ensure appropriate succession planning for the role of chair;
  - be present at the AGM and any EGM; and
  - attend regular shareholder meetings and/or analyst briefings to gauge a balanced view of their issues and concerns, particularly if the company has any activist shareholders.
- The FRC Guidance on Board Effectiveness additionally suggests the following in paragraph 68:

  > When the board or company is undergoing a period of stress, the SID's role becomes critically important. They are expected to work with the chair and other directors, and/or shareholders, to resolve significant issues. Boards should ensure they have a clear understanding of when the SID might intervene in order to maintain board and company stability. Examples might include where:
  >
  > - there is a dispute between the chair and chief executive;
  > - shareholders or NEDs have expressed concerns that are not being addressed by the chair or chief executive;
  > - the strategy is not supported by the entire board;
  > - the relationship between the chair and chief executive is particularly close;
  > - decisions are being made without the approval of the full board;
  > - succession planning is being ignored.

Further information

- FRC: Higgs Review (2003).
- FRC: UK Corporate Governance Code (2018).
- FRC: Guidance on Board Effectiveness 2018.

Shareholders

Introduction

A shareholder is a person, company or institution that owns at least one share in a company.

The shares, together with other funds which may from time to time accrue to the shareholders (e.g. share premiums, retained profits asset revaluation reserves) are jointly known as the equity of the company. In a straight-form balance sheet the equity of the company will balance with (be equal to) the net assets of the company.

The ownership of one or more shares brings two main rights:

- the right to vote at a general meeting of the company in proportion to the percentage of shares owned; and
- the right to a share of any dividend or other distribution made by the company to shareholders in proportion to the percentage of shares owned.

Shares are often acquired in the anticipation that the value of the share will increase allowing a profit to be made on the capital investment through selling of the share(s).

- In a listed company, the share price is easily identifiable from the exchange where the shares of that company are traded.
- In a private company, the value of a share is the subject of much greater speculation and calculation, often based on a formula include in the constitution of the company or an additional agreement between shareholders.

It is important for the directors of a company to have a good relationship with their shareholders. They are the providers of core underpinning capital within the company.

The reputation of a listed company can be significantly affected by the opinions and decisions of the shareholders. Reputation, the ability to obtain bank and other funding, and relationships with other stakeholders is often aligned to the quantum and movements of the share price of the company. This is only ever determined by whether there is a move by shareholders to buy or sell shares on the market.

Provision three of the UK Corporate Governance Code suggests:

> In addition to formal general meetings, the chair should seek regular engagement with major shareholders in order to understand their views on governance and performance against the strategy. Committee chairs should seek engagement with shareholders on significant matters related to their areas of responsibility. The chair should ensure that the board as a whole has a clear understanding of the views of shareholders.

In a world of increased shareholder activism, particularly around issues such as director remuneration, corporate social responsibility and workforce engagement, it is increasingly important for directors to maintain a keen awareness of the opinions of their shareholders.

Relationship with shareholders is a two-way process and paragraph 36 of the 2018 FRC Guidance on Board Effectiveness suggests:

> It is important that all shareholders are able to discharge their stewardship duties effectively. Formal ways of doing this are shareholder meetings and the AGM.

Paragraph 37 recognises the danger of an over-emphasis on major shareholders, stating:

> Smaller investors can be overlooked when board focus is primarily on major shareholders. Boards may want to consider additional ways to engage with smaller shareholders, for example, by methods of group engagement such as shareholder roundtables or webinars.

NED checklist

- Do you have an analysis of the shareholding of the company?
- Are you aware of the views and opinions of shareholders?
- Are you, as a NED, encouraged to meet with shareholders?
- Is there an appropriate level of constructive communication with large major and minor shareholders? Remember that it is a duty of a director to ensure that all shareholders are treated equally.

Notes

- Shareholders are always classed financially as a 'liability' of the business. If the business was to close, with assets being sold and liabilities paid, the net cash asset remaining would be owed to the shareholders of the business and would be distributed in proportion to their shareholding.
- In its corporate governance policy and voting guidelines, the Pensions and Lifetime Savings Association advocates constructive dialogue between companies and their shareholders, as a means of effective and responsible ownership. Its policy states:

For this dialogue to be most effective it should take place throughout the year, rather than being compressed into the period leading up to the shareholder meeting. Both companies and investors should be prepared and equipped to have intelligent, holistic conversations about the business and its strategy and how governance arrangements support this.

Single Alternative Inspection Location (SAIL)

Introduction

As an alternative to keeping all statutory records at the registered office of the company, such records can be kept at a Single Alternative Inspection Location. This is referred to as the SAIL address.

A SAIL address must be a location that is suitable for inspection of statutory records as and if required and authorised. There can only be one such alternative address which must be in the part of the UK in which the company is registered.

NED checklist

- Are any or all the statutory registers or documents kept at a SAIL address?
- Is the location adequate for the inspection of records?
- Are the inspection processes clear and appropriate for the type and size of company?
- Is a record kept of when records are inspected and by whom? Is this available to the directors of the company?

Procedure

- Directors must agree to the use of a SAIL location and agree which records will be kept there.
- Companies House must be notified of any records kept at the SAIL location.

Further information

- Companies House guidance.

Stakeholders

Introduction

Section 172 of CA2006 requires the directors of a company, through statutory duty, to promote the success of the company over the long term for the benefit of shareholders as a whole, having regard to a range of other key stakeholder interests.

For accounting periods beginning on or after 1 January 2019, companies classed as large under CA2006 are required to provide an explanation in their strategic report of how they have fulfilled their duty to stakeholders.

Paragraph 41 of the 2018 FRC Guidance on Board Effectiveness states:

> An effective board understands that a company has to engage with its workforce and build and maintain relationships with suppliers, customers and others in order to be successful over the long term. It will be able to explain how those relationships contribute to that success and help deliver the company's purpose. The company's approach to stakeholder engagement will be an important topic in the induction programme for new directors.

Paragraph 42 suggests:

> Dialogue with stakeholders can help boards to understand significant changes in the landscape, predict future developments and trends, and re-align strategy . Boards will find it useful to start by identifying and prioritising those key stakeholders who are important in the context of their business.

NED checklist

- Have you identified all your key stakeholders? Who they are, their views and opinions? How have you done this and is it up to date?
- Have stakeholder interests and influences been prioritised and do you understand their varying levels of power?

- Do the board discuss, on a regular basis, the key concerns of core stakeholder groups – workforce, suppliers, customers, providers of finance?
- Do you consider the stakeholder voice in your strategic decision making?
- As a board do you consider how environmental and social issues might impact upon your business and our reputation?
- Is the company's approach to stakeholder engagement included in the induction programme for new directors?
- Are the NEDs encouraged to meet with stakeholders on a regular basis?

Procedure

- Identify the core stakeholder groups for an organisation. These are often split into four categories:
  - Members: the shareholders, those who own the net assets of the company.
  - Employees: those who give their time and effort to the operation of the company.
  - Suppliers and customers: those who sell to and buy from the company.
  - Community and environment: those impacted by the wider societal activities of the company.
- Use a mapping tool to consider the expectations of the stakeholders. An example of such a tool would be as follows, but it is important for directors to find a tool that is directly appropriate to their particular business and set of stakeholders.

Stakeholder	Primary expectations	Secondary expectations
Owners (internal)	Financial return	Added value
Employees (internal)	Pay	Work satisfaction, training
Customers (market)	Supply of goods and services	Quality
Creditors (market)	Creditworthiness	Payment on time
Suppliers (market)	Payment	Long-term relationships
Community (external)	Safety and security	Contribution to community
Government (external)	Compliance	Improved competitiveness

- Another approach is to analyse stakeholders into different categories of levels of interest, and levels of power. Again, by way of example:

STAKEHOLDER MAPPING	Low interest in the business	High interest in the business
Low power to disrupt the business	Minimal effort required by the organisation	Stakeholders must be kept informed
High power to disrupt the business	Stakeholders must be kept satisfied	These are the key players

Further information

- The Chartered Governance Institute: guidance note, 'The stakeholder voice in board decision making'.
- FRC: Guidance on Board Effectiveness (2018).

Strategic report

Introduction

In 2013, the first major revision to the Companies Act 2006 was enacted with regard to reporting. The main effect was to remove s. 417 from the original Act, which contained all the reporting requirements contained in the EU Accounts Modernisation Directive and replace it with a new s. 414A.

Much of the wording is similar, but the core driver was to require directors to produce, with effect from 1 October 2013, a strategic report while continuing to require a directors' report (s. 415). Further changes to the expectations for stakeholder alignment, as identified below, have been enacted to take effect from accounting periods commencing on or after 1 January 2019.

Section 415 of CA2006 now requires the directors of limited companies (other than companies classified as a 'small company' or as a 'micro-entity') to provide a strategic report for each financial year of the company.

The report will form part of the annual report and accounts that are submitted to Companies House. Failure to provide such a report as and when required is an offence under the Act, committed by every person who was a director immediately before the end of the period for filing of report and accounts for the financial year in question.

NED checklist

- Has the latest strategic report for the current year end been reviewed and considered in the light of changes in the company during the year?
- Do the NEDs discuss and see the strategic report early enough in the reporting process? Remember that this report is made on a statutory basis in the name of all directors, so NEDs must be satisfied that the words represent your individual and collective views.
- Does the strategic report contain all statutory requirements?
- Do the words align with the figures included in the annual report?

- Although remuneration reporting falls outside the direct expectations of the strategic report, it is increasingly important that strategy can be seen to be aligned with remuneration.
- Does the strategic report help give a clear and appropriate picture of the culture of the organisation?

Requirements

- The relationship between the strategic report and s. 172 of CA2006 is stated as:

  > The purpose of the strategic report is to inform members of the company and help them assess how the directors have performed their duty under section 172 (duty to promote the success of the company).

- This expectation was enhanced by the Companies (Miscellaneous Reporting) Regulations 2018 which added a new requirement for all companies classed as large companies under CA2006. This added a new s. 414CZA to CA2006:

  > A strategic report for a financial year of a company must include a statement (a "section 172(1) statement") which describes how the directors have had regard to the matters set out in section 172(1)(a) to (f) when performing their duty under section 172.

- In addition, the strategic report must contain:
  - a fair review of business;
  - a balanced and comprehensive analysis of performance (income statement) and position (balance sheet) consistent with size and complexity;
  - a description of principal risks and uncertainties; and
  - the key performance indicators (KPIs) that are used to measure and identify success and performance within the company; large companies are required to include non-financial KPIs in addition to financial KPIs.
- Listed companies are also required to include:
  - a description of the company's strategy;
  - a description of the company's business model; and
  - an employee analysis showing gender split at director, senior manager and employee level.
- The strategic report must be approved by the board of directors and signed by a director or the secretary.

Notes

- The strategic report replaces the requirement for summary financial statements.
- The strategic report can act as a standalone document for shareholders who do not wish to receive the full annual report.
- A large company under the Act is defined as one that satisfies two out of three of the following criteria:
  - a turnover of more than £36 million;
  - a balance sheet of more than £18 million; and
  - more than 250 employees.
- Reminder of s.172 of CA2006:

  A director of a company must act in the way he considers, in good faith, would be most likely to promote the success of the company for the benefit of its members as a whole and in doing so have regard (amongst other matters) to:

  a) the likely consequences of any decision in the long term,

  b) the interest of the company's employees,

  c) the need to foster the company's business relationships with suppliers, customers and others,

  d) the impact of the company's operations on the community and the environment

  e) the desirability of the company maintaing a reputation for high standards of business conduct, and

  f) the need to act fairly as between members of the company.

Further information

- The Companies Act 2006.

Strategy alignment

Introduction

A core focus of effective governance is the alignment of strategy with risk and control as stated in Principle O of the 2018 UK Corporate Governance Code:

> The board should establish procedures to manage risk, oversee the internal control framework, and determine the nature and extent of the principal risks the company is willing to take in order to achieve its long-term strategic objectives.

This wording is very similar to that used within the 2016 Code, the only material difference being the addition of the words 'long-term' bringing this principle into alignment with the duties of directors included in s.172 of CA2006.

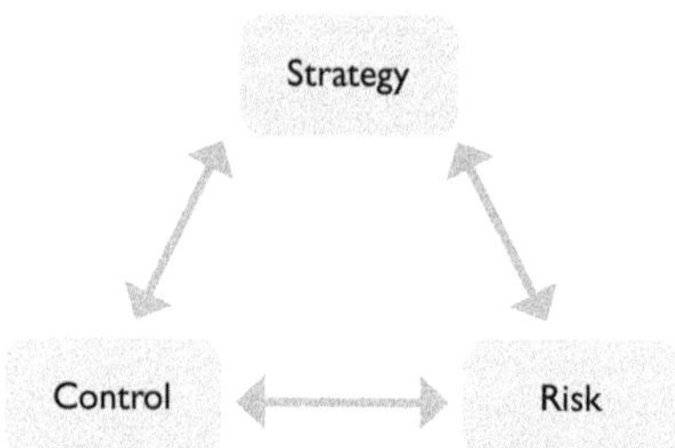

This triangulation requires directors to step back from the immediacy of the modern-day and take time to reflect, consider, debate and challenge what is actually happening in their organisation, and whether strategic changes are required.

Those empowered with governance need to understand the strategic objectives of the organisation, the risks associated with the achievement of those objectives and how to then control and mitigate the identified risks.

Principle B of the UK Corporate Governance Code states:

> The boards should establish the company's purpose, values and strategy, and satisfy itself that these and its culture are aligned.

NED checklist

- Does the board agenda allow for sufficient and appropriate discussion of strategy, strategic direction and strategic objectives?
- As directors, do you challenge and debate how you ensure that appropriate controls exist to mitigate the risk associated with your strategy?
- Given the CA2006 expectation of the 'promotion of success' do you, as directors and as a board, understand what strategic success looks like for your organisation?
- How do we measure progress towards achieving these strategic objectives?

Procedure

- Develop a strategic plan for the company, and regularly review and update.
- Strategy: set the direction. This is the remit and expectation of the directors of a company.
- Risk: recognise the dangers that exist along the strategic route. The decisions of directors and others will 'risk' the assets, wealth and reputation of the organisation.
- Control: establish appropriate control, oversight and review measures, so that assurances can be given by the board to shareholders.

Further information

- Checklists: Balanced scorecard (page 26) and Key performance indicators (page 179).

Strategy development

Introduction

The UK Corporate Governance Code states:

> Principle A
>
> 'A successful company is led by an effective and entrepreneurial board, whose role is to promote the long-term sustainable success of the company, generating value for shareholders and contributing to wider society.'
>
> Principle B
>
> 'The board should establish the company's purpose, values and strategy.'

The setting of strategy is right at the centre of the requirements from any board of directors. They are accountable to the shareholders of the company for delivering success (CA2006 s. 172) and this will not be achieved by chance.

Students taking The Chartered Governance Institute's 'Development of Strategy' paper are advised to visually contemplate how strategy needs to develop:

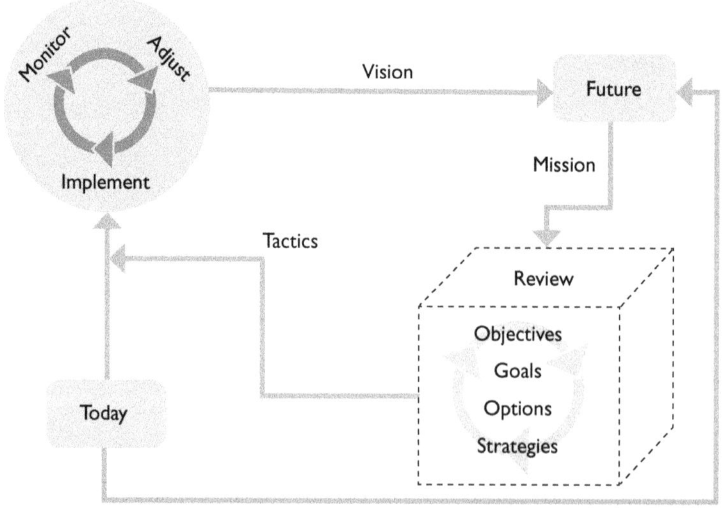

Strategy starts at 'today' and works towards the 'future'. The past has already happened: we can learn from it, but we cannot change it. Every organisation 'today' is implementing, monitoring or adjusting the plans from the past.

The role of those empowered with the development of strategy, the directors of the company is to develop a vision of what might change or needs to change for the 'future' and then take themselves and the organisation through the necessary thinking and challenge iterations to redesign what is happening 'today'.

- This thinking applies to long-term strategy – Should we enter a new marketplace?
- It also applies to short-term strategy – How can we deliver a benefit this year for our shareholders?

Paragraph 16 of the FRC Guidance on Board Effectiveness suggests:

> Diversity of skills, background and personal strengths is an important driver of a board's effectiveness, creating different perspectives among directors, and breaking down a tendency towards 'group think.

That same guidance suggests that NEDs should:

- 'visit operations and talk with managers and non-managerial members of the workforce'
- 'better understand the culture of the organisation'
- 'receive high-quality information'
- 'not operate exclusively in the confines of the boardroom'
- 'meet shareholders, key customers and members of the workforce'.

In this and other ways, the NED can bring an informed, objective and independent challenge to the strategic vision and objectives of the business.

NED checklist

- How does the company approach and discuss strategy? At a specific meeting once a year separate and distinct from a normal board meeting? Does strategy appear regularly on the board agenda? Do you feel as a NED, you contribute sufficiently to the strategy debate and formulation?
- Do you understand the business well enough to share of the vision of how and why it could change, or needs to change?
- Does your board discuss strategy on an on going basis and consider this when discussing regular board agenda items? Is there sufficient time to do this in board meetings?

- When and what was the last material contribution that you, as a NED, made to the strategic aims of the executive directors? They spend their life thinking about this business. You have the independence, separation and objectivity to be able to place those strategic aims within the wider macro-economic world where we are required to exist, survive and continue to deliver success.

Further information

- The Chartered Governance Institute: study text, Development of Strategy (2019).
- FRC: Guidance on Board Effectiveness (2018).
- FRC: UK Corporate Governance Code (2018).

Subsidiary companies

Introduction

A company is a subsidiary of another company, its holding company, if that company:

- holds a majority of the voting rights in it; or
- is a member of it and has the right to appoint or remove a majority of its board of directors; or
- is a member of it and controls alone, pursuant to an agreement with other members, a majority of the voting rights in it; or
- if it is a subsidiary of a company, that is itself a subsidiary of that other company.

A company becomes a wholly owned subsidiary if the holding or parent company owns all the shares by itself or through the holding company's nominees. A holding company and its subsidiaries are collectively called a group. The importance of this classification relates to:

- the requirement to publish group accounts (i.e. consolidated accounts which reflect the performance of both the holding company and all the subsidiary companies);
- financial assistance in the purchase of shares: a holding company may help in the purchase of shares in its subsidiary but not vice versa;
- the avoidance of provisions on fair dealing by directors: for example, provisions on loans to directors do not apply when the loan is to a director of a subsidiary company;
- the increase in limited liability: a major company law consideration favouring the use of subsidiaries is the increased level of limited liability afforded to the group as a whole. Valuable assets such as group freehold properties might, for example, be transferred to a non-trading group company, or a high-risk trading activity carried on within a subsidiary which has no other activities.

NED checklist

- Does the company have any subsidiary companies or a parent?
- Are you a director of the parent company or a subsidiary? If a director of a subsidiary company what is the position of the company within the group?
- Are the directors of subsidiary companies the same as the directors of the holding/or parent company?
- Even if a NED is not a serving director of a subsidiary, that NED will be considered to have legal oversight of activities of the subsidiary by virtue of being a NED of the holding company.

Trading while insolvent

Introduction

If a business continues to trade while insolvent, the directors of the business can become personally liable to contribute to the assets of the company and could be faced with a fine, imprisonment and/or a disqualification order.

This liability is explicitly extended to all directors of a limited company including de facto directors and shadow directors.

An insolvent company does not need to be deemed as indefinitely insolvent. At times, problems of short-term insolvency might be driven by customers not paying on time. If the money owed to the company exceeds its liabilities, an investigation would be likely to show that there was no intent by the directors to act irresponsibly.

However, a company that simply cannot and will never be able to pay its creditors in a timely manner is likely to be found guilty of wrongful trading. The presumption here will be that the directors know that their company is insolvent and have no plans of how they will pay their creditors. It is unacceptable for directors to continue trading knowing that they are worsening the position of their creditors and building further debt within the company.

NED checklist

- Do the directors receive regular accurate and timely management accounts, in particular, reflecting the liquidity and solvency of the business?
- Are the accounting records of the business up to date and transparent?
- Does the information provided enable the directors to ascertain whether the assets exceed the liabilities and that the company is able to pay its liabilities when they fall due?
- Do the directors regularly monitor the liquidity position of the business, particularly at times of financial stress?

- If uncertain as to the liquidity and ongoing viability of the business, are all financial transactions be considered with due care and attention?
- If you believe that the business is insolvent, resignation will not negate your liability, and external professional advice from an insolvency practitioner should be obtained at the earliest opportunity.

Procedure

- The Insolvency Act 1986 seeks to determine:
  - Do the liabilities of the company exceed the assets?
  - Is the company able to pay their liabilities as they fall due?
- Section 123 of the Insolvency Act 1986 applies some specific criteria to the declaring of insolvency:
  - if a creditor who is owed over £750 has served on the company's registered office a statutory demand requiring the company to pay the sum due and the company has for three weeks neglected to pay the sum, secure or compound it;
  - if in England and Wales, execution or other process issued on a judgment, decree, order of any court is returned unsatisfied in whole, or in part;
  - if it is proved to the satisfaction of the court that the company is unable to pay its debts, as they fall due; and
  - if the value of the company's assets is less than the amount of its liabilities, taking into account its contingent and prospective liabilities.

If a company is declared insolvent, a wrongful trading action can be brought against the directors. To be found guilty of the offence, the court will need to believe that the officer of the company ought to have concluded that the company had no realistic prospect of avoiding insolvent liquidation.

Further, that if the company's debts have increased and additional liabilities have been incurred when there is no prospect of the debts being met, it will be presumed that the director knew or ought to have concluded that there was no reasonable prospect that the company could avoid going into insolvent liquidation.

Training and development

Introduction

A director will usually participate in an induction programmes at the start of their term of office. This should be proportionate with the size and complexity of the business, and designed to introduce and explain the culture, finances, risks, reporting, procedures, operational activities, and other pertinent matters relating to the business.

This will enable the new director to participate in the governance of the business and other associated NED duties and expectations.

The most useful ongoing training and development is the type that varies with circumstances and individuals; however, the objective of any such process should be to improve the skill set of each NED in a way that is relevant to the individual.

The human experience is one of perpetual learning so very often the more a person finds out, the more a person wants to know. In a board of directors this can often be a mutual or two-way experience.

- An individual director will want to know and understand more to better fulfil their role.
- The changing requirements of the organisation and/or the mixture of directors might require one or more directors to learn new skills.

NED checklist

- Does a director training and development programme exist?
- Does the company budget for director training and development?
- Does the chair discuss training and development with each director to ascertain an individual's needs and/or with the board as a whole to ascertain the board's requirements?
- Is there an appropriate and robust annual board and director evaluation process to help to identify training and development needs?

Procedure

- Training and development needs will usually be identified in one of three ways:
  - the individual director recognises and asks for particular development;
  - the chair recognises a gap in an individual or group skillset; and
  - the board and director evaluation process identifies the need for further training and development.
- The company secretary will often oversee the logistics and arrangement of appropriate agreed training for each director and/or for the board as a whole.
- Training and development may take many forms (classroom-style training, one-to-one training or bulletins), it may be achieved through on going updates on regulations, law, governance, risk trends and developments or be technical in nature (e.g. relating to finance).

UK Corporate Governance Code

Introduction

The first version of a UK corporate governance code was published in 1992. Its title was 'The Financial Aspects of Corporate Governance'. It was the final report of a committee led by Sir Adrian Cadbury and convened by the government of the day to consider how companies might be better overseen by their directors on behalf of their shareholders. As with many such reviews and committees, this followed several corporate failures and scandals (Polly Peck and Maxwell/Trinity Mirror in particular).

This initial attempt at a code was followed rapidly by a plethora of different committees considering different aspects of corporate governance, resulting in the FRC issuing a 'Combined Code of Corporate Governance' and then eventually 'the UK Corporate Governance Code' (the Code).

The strength of the Code is its adoption by the London Stock Exchange and the Listing Rule requirements that companies with a public listing of their shares are required to follow the expectations of the Code on a 'comply or explain' basis. They either comply with the Code or explain within their report and accounts why they do not.

The latest iteration is the UK Corporate Governance Code 2018. The FRC identify the main changes as being related to:

- Workforce and stakeholders – the need for greater engagement and disclosure.
- Culture – an alignment of company values, strategy and long-term value preservation.
- Succession and diversity – a reconsideration of how to achieve an optimal board today and in the future.
- Remuneration – the expectation that executive remuneration will be set within a broad context.

The FRC also claim that the 2018 Code is 'shorter and sharper'.

It is technically shorter, although there are more cross-references now to other FRC guidance documents, such as the 2018 Guidance on Board Effectiveness. The section on audit has been reduced by placing more reliance on the FRC Guidance for Audit Committees.

Is it sharper? The current FRC structure gives it only limited powers to demand change from companies, but the proposed transition to the new Audit, Reporting and Governance Authority (ARGA) will see the creation of a sharper regulated structure with power delegated from the UK government.

NED checklist

- Are we required to comply with the UK Corporate Governance Code?
- If yes:
  - Has this been discussed around the board table, or is it just treated as an assumption?
  - Are you satisfied, as a NED, that the governance reporting is accurate and compliant in all aspects?
  - Have you read the Code and considered its implications?
- If no:
  - Read a copy of the Code and consider how your company handles its governance – just because you don't have to do something, it doesn't mean that you shouldn't be aligning to perceived best practice.

Requirements

- The Code is applicable to all companies with a premium listing on the London Stock Exchange and applies to accounting periods beginning on or after 1 January 2019.
- Many other companies and organisations either aspire to or state that they intend to be compliant with the UK Code. All listed UK companies, now including AIM companies, are expected to comply with a governance code, and the majority opt for the FRC UK Code.

Further information

- FRC: The UK Corporate Governance Code (2018).

Wates Principles of Corporate Governance

Introduction

In 2016, the UK Government, acting through the Department of Business Energy and Industrial Strategy (BEIS) issued a Green Paper on corporate governance reform, with the purpose of reviewing the governance expectation and requirement within the corporate private sector. Prior to this, in the UK corporate world, the only official required formulation of governance applied to companies with shares listed on the London Stock Exchange. These companies were required to follow the expectations of the UK Corporate Governance Code, now in its 2018 iteration.

The green paper consultation led the establishment of a working party coalition group to be led by James Wates to consider how best to develop corporate governance principles for large private companies. The perceived need for enhanced private company governance was driven by:

- evidence of governance failings in a number of high-profile public corporate collapses;
- a greater stakeholder awareness and demand for information, leading to more significant stakeholder expectations;
- the gap that exists between short-term and long-term corporate perspectives – survival versus strategy;
- a perceived widening of a lack of trust in UK business;
- the ratcheting of pay levels and, in particular, the perceived misalignment of executive and workforce pay; and
- the need for more accuracy and transparency in corporate reporting.

Following an initial consultation in June 2018, the resultant Wates Corporate Governance Principles for Large Private Companies were released in December 2018 to be effective from financial periods starting on or after 1 January 2019, and to be applicable to a new tier of large private companies that satisfy either or both of the following criteria:

- more than 2,000 employees
- a turnover of more than £200 million, and a balance sheet of more than £2 billion.

NED checklist

- Determine whether your organisation falls within the parameters of expectation for application of the Wates principles.
- If yes: ensure that the principles and how you are going to address them are debated around the board table and that there is a firm (not just tacit) plan of action. The principles are designed to form a governance culture, not just a reporting requirement.
- If not: challenge and encourage your fellow directors to consider 'Why would we not want to apply these principles'?

The six Wates principles

- *Principle 1: Purpose and leadership*

  An effective board develops and promotes the purpose of a company, and ensures that its values, strategy and culture align with that purpose.

- *Principle 2: Board composition*

  Effective board composition requires an effective chair and a balance of skills, backgrounds, experience and knowledge, with individual directors having sufficient capacity to make a valuable contribution. The size of a board should be guided by the scale and complexity of the company.

- *Principle 3: Director responsibilities*

  The board and individual directors should have a clear understanding of their accountability and responsibilities. The board's policies and procedures should support effective decision-making and independent challenge.

- *Principle 4: Opportunity and risk*

  A board should promote the long-term sustainable success of the company by identifying opportunities to create and preserve value and establishing oversight for the identification and mitigation of risks.

- *Principle 5: Remuneration*

  A board should promote executive remuneration structures aligned to the long-term sustainable success of a company, taking into account pay and conditions elsewhere in the company.

- *Principle 6: Stakeholder relationships and engagement*

  Directors should foster effective stakeholder relationships aligned to the company's purpose. The board is responsible for overseeing meaningful engagement with stakeholders, including the workforce and having regard to their views when taking decisions.

Requirements

- The Wates principles are to be applied on an 'apply and explain' basis, as opposed to the 'comply or explain' principle that underpins the UK Code.
- This is taking a slightly different approach by suggesting that all companies covered by this new regime should be required to apply these principles within the governance of their organisation and explain how they have so applied them, or if they have not applied them, then why not?

Notes

- Comment from James Wates on the release of the principles:

  > I believe that good business, well done, is a force for good in society.
  >
  > The Wates Corporate Governance Principles are a tool for large private companies that helps them look themselves in the mirror, to see where they've done well, and where they can raise their corporate governance standards to a higher level.
  >
  > Good corporate governance is not about box-ticking. It can only be achieved if companies think seriously about why they exist and how they deliver on their purpose then explain – in their own words – how they go about implementing the principles. That's the sort of transparency that can build the trust of stakeholders and the general public.

Further information

- The Wates Corporate Governance Principles for Large Private Companies (2018).

Whistleblowing

Introduction

Whistleblowing can be defined as the disclosure by a person, often an employee, of actual or perceived mismanagement, corruption, illegality or some other wrongdoing. The disclosure could be to those in authority within an organisation, to an external authority or regulator or to the media or public as a whole.

Companies covered by the UK Corporate Governance Code, and many other companies who form part of a sector network, are required to have a 'whistleblowing policy' which identifies the means through which an employee, or another informed and/or interested person, can safely make such a disclosure without fear of retribution.

Section 57 of the FRC Guidance on Board Effectiveness 2018 states:

> Having policies in place that encourage individuals to raise concerns is a core part of an ethical and supportive business culture. Whistleblowing policies that offer effective protection from retaliation, as well as policies that support anti bribery and corruption legislation are essential components of this. Such policies are important, for example, when attempts to resolve things internally have not worked.

In earlier versions of the UK Corporate Governance Code, responsibility for the establishment and monitoring of whistleblowing policies was included under the expectations of the audit committee. In the 2018 Code, the responsibility has been moved into the first section (Board Leadership and Company Purpose) reflecting the increased perceived importance of clarity of communication with the workforce of an organisation. Provision 6 of the 2018 Code states:

> There should be a means for the workforce to raise concerns in confidence and – if they wish – anonymously. The board should routinely review this and the reports arising from its operation. It should ensure that arrangements are in place for the proportionate and independent investigation of such matters and for follow-up action.

NED checklist

- Is there a clear, accessible and well-defined communication process for whistleblowing within the organisation?
- If this does not exist, investigate why not and recommend its establishment as soon as appropriate.
- How are employees and others made aware of this process?
- How is the process monitored? How are matters raised under the process handled within the organisation?
- Do directors receive a regular report of any disclosures made under such a process? Is there an appropriate discussion amongst directors?
- If no disclosures have been made, consider at board level whether this means the whistleblowing procedure is ineffective or if this reflects the fact there are no issues. The board needs to be mindful of the fact that whistleblowing is a governance risk. Therefore, having a suitable system in place is essential, to protect the company, the individual(s) and stakeholders.
- As a NED, do you have confidence that any such whistleblowing process is controlled and operated in an appropriate manner for the size and type of organisation, ensuring that any person making such a disclosure is not subject to any retaliation or retribution from the organisation, or from those in authority within the organisation?

Procedure

- Read the whistleblowing procedure for the organisation.
- Assess the appropriateness of the procedure for the size, type and nature of the organisation and its stakeholders.
- Investigate whether there have been any disclosures made under the whistleblowing process and ensure that any such disclosures have been handled in an appropriate, confidential and resolutory manner.

Winding up of a company

Introduction

The process of dissolving a limited company is known as winding up the company. During the process of winding up, a company must cease to carry out any further business other than to sell inventory, pay creditors, and distribute any remaining assets to its members.

The term liquidation is often used synonymously with the phrase winding up as a description of the process of the liquidation of any assets of the company. However, neither term implies that the company is illiquid or bankrupt, although the process of liquidation or winding up will almost always follow a state of bankruptcy.

A winding-up process can be initiated voluntarily by the shareholders of a company when they believe there is no further purpose in the continuation of that company. Alternatively, a winding-up process can be brought into legal force by a court order, usually initiated by the company's creditors, including, but not restricted to, one or more banks or other lenders or HMRC with regard to non-payment of taxes.

NED Checklist

- If a decision is taken to wind up the main company where you are a NED, or one of its subsidiary companies, ensure that you are aware of any provisions under the articles of association of the company with regard to your role or rights as a director.
- If the company is being wound up as the result of a court order, have you taken every legal and potential step to ensure that you will not hold any liability for the debts of the company?
- If you have any doubt over your role or liability within the winding up of a company or its subsidiary, it is advisable to seek appropriate legal advice. In the case of the winding up of a subsidiary company, it would be reasonable to expect the main company to pay for such legal advice.
- Is any potential legal action against you as a director covered by directors and officers (D&O) liability insurance?

Workforce engagement

Introduction

In their launch of the 2018 UK Corporate Governance Code, the FRC recognised that there was a political drive and a societal expectation of a greater engagement between a company's directors and its workforce and other stakeholders.

Principle E of the Code states:

> The board should ensure that workforce policies and practices are consistent with the company's values and support its long-term sustainable success. The workforce should be able to raise any matters of concern.

This is supported by provision five of the Code which states:

> For engagement with the workforce, one or a combination of the following methods should be used.
>
> - a director appointed from the workforce
> - a formal workforce advisory panel
> - a designated non-executive director.
>
> If the board has not chosen one or more of these methods, it should explain what alternative arrangements are in place and why it considers that they are effective.

Although these are strictly only requirements for companies who are required to comply with the Code, the intention an expectation should be clear for directors of all companies. As part of their duty under s. 172 of CA2006, directors must increase and enhance their engagement with the employees of the company as key stakeholders.

NED checklist

- Are employees of the organisation treated as a strategic asset?
- Has the organisation embedded its values and expected behaviours within the human resource policies, processes and practices?

- Is the level of engagement with the workforce appropriate and frequent enough, with the size and complexity of the organisation?
- Are you encouraged to 'walk the floor' of the business and engage in conversation with employees?
- Is the organisation doing enough to train and develop its employees with the skills they will need for the future?
- Does the board of directors have a formalised and regular method for the genuine and honest views of the workforce to be considered around the board table?

Notes

- A board of directors may feel it is inappropriate to adopt one of the three methods suggested by the Code for formal engagement with the workforce. It is up to each company to develop an appropriate and meaningful method for such engagement. A company obliged to comply with the code will be able to fulfil this requirement by explaining how a meaningful and regular dialogue takes place.
- If a director is appointed from the workforce to bring a workforce view to the board-room, that person will have the same duties and responsibilities as the other directors under CA2006. Their role is not to represent solely the views of the workforce, so training and support will be critical for this director to ensure that they understand the wider aspects of company finance and business decision making and are able to work with the other directors, contributing to discussions on the wider strategic demands of the business.

Further information

- FRC: Guidance on Board Effectiveness (2018).

Web directory

Advisory, Conciliation and Arbitration Service
www.acas.org.uk

Bar Council
www.barcouncil.org.uk

British and Irish Legal Information Institute
www.bailii.org

Chartered Institute of Management Accountants
www.cimaglobal.com

Chartered Institute of Legal Executives
www.cilex.org.uk

Companies House
www.gov.uk/government/organisations/companies-house

Company information
beta.companieshouse.gov.uk/

Company name checker
beta.companieshouse.gov.uk/company-name-availability

Competition & Markets Authority
www.gov.uk/government/organisations/competition-and-markets-authority

Confederation of British Industry
www.cbi.org.uk/

Court of Justice of the European Union
curia.europa.eu

Courts and Tribunals Judiciary
www.judiciary.gov.uk

Department for Business, Energy & Industrial Strategy
www.gov.uk/government/organisations/department-for-business-energy-and-industrial-strategy

Domain name registrars
ICANN
www.icann.org

Nominet UK
www.nominet.uk

Internic
www.internic.net

European Business Registry Association
https://ebra.be

European Court of Human Rights
echr.coe.int

European Patent Office
www.epo.org/

European Union
https://europa.eu

Financial Conduct Authority
FCA Handbook
www.handbook.fca.org.uk/handbook

Listing rules
www.handbook.fca.org.uk/handbook/LR/

Financial Services Register
register.fca.org.uk/

Mutuals Public Register
www.fca.org.uk/firms/mutuals-public-register

Primary Markets
www.fca.org.uk/markets/primary-markets

Financial Reporting Council
www.frc.org.uk

Audit resources
www.frc.org.uk/auditors

Corporate governance
www.frc.org.uk/directors/corporate-governance-and-stewardship

HM Courts & Tribunals Service
www.gov.uk/government/organisations/hm-courts-and-tribunals-service

HM Land Registry
www.gov.uk/government/organisations/land-registry

HM Revenue & Customs
www.gov.uk/government/organisations/hm-revenue-customs

Stamp duty
www.gov.uk/topic/business-tax/stamp-taxes

Information Commissioner's Office
www.ico.org.uk

Institute of Chartered Accountants in England and Wales
www.icaew.com

Institute of Chartered Accountants in Ireland
www.charteredaccountants.ie

Institute of Chartered Accountants in Scotland
www.icas.com

Institute of Directors
www.iod.com

Intellectual Property Office
www.gov.uk/government/organisations/intellectual-property-office

International Corporate Governance Network
www.icgn.org

Judicial Committee of the Privy Council
www.jcpc.uk

Law society
www.lawsociety.org.uk

London Stock Exchange
www.londonstockexchange.com/home/homepage.htm

Admission and disclosure standards
www.londonstockexchange.com/companies-and-advisors/main-market/documents/admission-and-disclosure-standards.pdf

AIM rules
www.londonstockexchange.com/companies-and-advisors/aim/publications/rules-regulations/rules-regulations.htm

Dividend timetable
www.londonstockexchange.com/traders-and-brokers/rules-regulations/dividend-procedure-timetable-2019.pdf

NEDonBoard
www.nedonboard.com

Non-Executive Directors' Association (NEDA)
www.nedaglobal.com

Pensions and Lifetime Savings Association
www.plsa.co.uk

Prudential Regulation Authority
www.bankofengland.co.uk/prudential-regulation

Supreme Court of the United Kingdom
www.supremecourt.uk

The Association of British Insurers
www.abi.org.uk

The Chartered Institute of Internal Auditors
www.iia.org.uk

The Chartered Governance Institute
www.icsa.org.uk/

Guidance material
www.icsa.org.uk/knowledge

Publications
www.icsa.org.uk/shop

The Institute of Business Ethics
www.ibe.org.uk

The Institute of Risk Management
www.theirm.org

The Quoted Companies Alliance
www.theqca.com

The Takeover Panel
www.thetakeoverpanel.org.uk

Trades Union Congress
www.tuc.org.uk

UK Legislation
www.legislation.gov.uk

UK Parliament
www.parliament.uk

Index

www.ingramcontent.com/pod-product-compliance
Ingram Content Group UK Ltd.
Pitfield, Milton Keynes, MK11 3LW, UK
UKHW021058130926
8556IPUK00046B/1218

9 781860 727931